ISRAEL - PALESTINE

WAR

Give Peace A Chance

DR. JOSEPH K THOMAS

Printed in India

ISBN: 978-93-6045-512-5

IndiePress

First Printing, 2024

Indie Press

A division of Nasadiya Technologies Private Ltd.
Koramangala, Bangalore
Karnataka-560029

http://indiepress.in/

Editor-Literary Connect
Typesetter - Parinkumar Nirmal
Book Cover Designer - Sankhusubhro Nath
Publishing Consultant - Anagha Somanakoppa

DEDICATIONS

To my parents, Mr. K V Thomas and Mrs. Mary Thomas, my wife, Helena, my son Daniel, and the rest of the family members.

To all the unsung heroes of our armed forces and Martyrs, for your supreme sacrifices to keep our country safe. Let us make ourselves worthy of their sacrifices.

INTRODUCTION

"*I*n the Middle East, the past is never dead. It's not even past." Borrowing from the immortal words of William Faulkner, this sentiment rings truer in the cradle of ancient civilizations than perhaps anywhere else on earth. It is here that history breathes in the winds, that every stone tells a story of faith, of struggle, of the unyielding yearning for a place to call home. What does it mean when the very land you stand on, is steeped in centuries of blood and belief, where every line in the soil has been turned by the toil of competing narratives? The Israeli-Palestinian war is not just the story of two peoples and the land they both claim, but an entanglement of historical, religious, and cultural complexities that has resisted untangling for generations.

The land, sacred to many, has been a crucible of civilization, a battleground for empires, and a fabric of cultures for millennia. A journey back through the corridors of time brings us to the birthplace of the three great monotheistic religions, each laying claim to this sliver of earth, a claim that has sparked countless conflicts and shaped the destinies of nations.

"In order to understand the geography of a place, one must first understand its history." Avi Shlaim, a renowned historian, encapsulates the essence of the land, that is both ancient and painfully current. This land, where olive trees have witnessed empires rise and fall, now trembles under the relentless rhythm of war drums. The Israeli-Palestinian war, a subject of my book, is not merely a matter of contested borders or political sovereignty; it is a profound testament to the human capacity for both tenacity and tragedy.

Shlaim's words serve as a beacon, guiding us through the corridors of the past, that lead the inevitable to the present. To unpack the meaning of his assertion is to acknowledge that the present landscape of conflict is but the latest layer atop the sediment of countless histories. The events that have unfolded are not sudden eruptions, but the result of pressures that have built up over decades, centuries even. This book is an endeavor to peel back those layers, to reveal the underlying currents that have shaped the contours of today's conflict.

At the heart of this conflict are two people, both with deep-seated claims to the same sliver of land. Both narratives are steeped in historical legitimacy, religious conviction, and an unquenchable thirst for a place to call their own. The challenge lies in reconciling these competing histories, which have been interwoven with the geography of the region in a manner that defies easy separation.

It is a common belief that wars are fought between armies, that they are matters of strategic objectives, territorial gains, and the assertion of strength. This perspective fails to capture the essence of the Israeli-Palestinian conflict. This is a war where the front lines are as likely to be in the hearts and minds of civilians as they are on the battlefield. It is a war where the boundaries between soldiers and citizens, between past and present, are blurred by the fog of shared grief and aspirations.

In the intricate collages of the Middle East, two

movements arose, almost concurrently, from the ashes of the Ottoman Empire, each embedded with the fervor of self-determination and the longing for statehood. Zionism, a Jewish national revival movement, and Arab nationalism, a call for unity and independence among Arab peoples, were both fuelled by the promise of sovereignty and the end of foreign domination. Their parallel ascents set the stage for a century of conflict, as dreams of national identity collided with the realities of overlapping territorial claims.

It is important to understand the motivations, aspirations, and historical context that gave rise to these two national movements. By examining their similarities and differences, we can gain insights into the complex dynamics that continue to shape the Israeli-Palestinian conflict. We will consider the historical origins, ideological foundations, and the evolution of both movements, as well as their impact on the geopolitical landscape of the region.

At their core, Zionism and Arab nationalism share remarkable similarities. Both sought to re-awaken a sense of pride and autonomy among people who had experienced subjugation. Theodor Herzl, often called the father of modern political Zionism, envisioned a Jewish state as a refuge from the rampant anti-Semitism of Europe. Similarly, Arab nationalists, inspired by figures like Sherif Hussein of Mecca, aimed to unite Arab lands under a single flag, free from Ottoman or Western control.

Zionism and Arab nationalism are not ancient relics, but living ideologies that continue to inspire, mobilize, and divide. As we delve into the depths of these movements, it becomes clear that the path to understanding the Israeli-Palestinian war is as complex as the narratives that drive it.

As much as their aspirations were alike, the divergence in their historical trajectories and territorial ambitions was stark. Zionism specifically focused on the ancient Jewish connection to the land of Israel, a narrow geographical locale with profound religious and historical significance for Jews worldwide. In contrast, Arab nationalism spanned a vast region from the Arabian Peninsula to North Africa, emphasizing linguistic and cultural unity among Arabs.

In the confluence of Zionism and Arab nationalism, we find not only the roots of conflict but perhaps the seeds of a future peace, one that acknowledges the intertwined destinies of Israelis and Palestinians. Can we, as witnesses to this age-old struggle, dare to envision a new chapter where these two narratives converge in a shared story of peace? Let us step forward with cautious optimism, for the road is long, and history has taught us that hope, though fragile, is the light that guides us through the darkness of discord.

The birth of Israel in 1948, following the United Nations partition plan, was a triumphant moment for Zionism, yet a catastrophic event for the Arab population of Palestine, known as the Nakba, or catastrophe. Here lies the crux of the distinction: for one group, the fulfillment of a long-held dream; for the other, the shattering of their own national aspirations on the very same soil.

How can we reconcile these two narratives, interwoven yet diametrically opposed? It was on the arid expanse of ancient lands that the origins of this conflict took root, with the formation of Israel in 1948 and the subsequent Arab-Israeli wars that carved deep scars into the collective memory of the region. The Six-Day War of 1967, with Israel's dramatic territorial gains, and the Yom Kippur War of 1973, which saw Arab nations launching a surprise attack on Yom Kippur, the holiest day in Judaism, are pivot points that have directly influenced the trajectory of the Israeli-Palestinian narrative.

The analysis of these movements reveals broader implications, especially in the way national identities are constructed, and the role external powers play in shaping regional destinies. It also sheds light on the persistent challenges in achieving a lasting peace when two national movements fight for legitimacy and sovereignty over the same land.

As dawn broke on the 7th of October 2023, a day that would be charred into the collective consciousness of a nation. The uneasy silence was shattered. Rockets tore through the sky, and the very earth seemed to tremble under the weight of an invasion no one saw coming. What followed would challenge the resolve of people and the world's understanding of war and peace in this sacred, scarred region.

How did we arrive at this juncture, where the promise of peace seems perennially out of reach? And where do we go from here, when the dust settles and the cries of the wounded are all that remain? Can there ever be a victor in a war, where the spoils are the broken hearts and shattered lives of the innocent? Before we can answer these questions, we must first bear witness to the events that transpired on that fateful morning of October 7, 2023, events that may well have rewritten the future of the Middle East.

In the shadow of the rockets' red glare, a new threat emerged, one that would test the resolve of a nation and the mettle of its people. This was not an assault from the skies, but a breach on the ground, a violent rupture of the seemingly unclear barrier that stood as a barricade between Gaza and Israel.

The barrier, a mix of concrete walls, fencing, and advanced surveillance technology, had long been a point of contention. To some, it was a necessary defense against infiltration and terror; to others, a symbol of division and despair. The morning after the rockets fell, it became the scene of a calculated incursion.

Militants, wielding tools and explosives with grim determination, had found a way through. The breach was not just a physical one; it was a tear in the fabric of security that many had taken for granted. As news of the breach spread, so did a palpable sense of vulnerability. If the barrier could be compromised, what was safe?

In the heart of a small community near the border, the sirens that once signaled incoming fire were now silent—the threat was already on their doorstep. Families who had weathered the storm of rockets now faced a new unknown. The militants' infiltration brought with it a sense of chaos, the kind that turns neighbor against neighbor in a frantic struggle for safety.

The breach of the Gaza-Israel barrier is a call to action—a plea for a future where barriers, both physical and metaphorical, are dismantled. It is a reminder that peace is not a passive state, but an active pursuit, one that requires courage, compassion, and the collective will to transcend the legacy of enmity. As the nation grappled with the breach's aftermath, the path ahead seemed fraught with uncertainty. Would there be retaliation, a tightening of restrictions, a further escalation of hostilities? Or could this moment of vulnerability become a catalyst for change?

The stakes were higher than ever. The breach of the Gaza-Israel barrier was not just an act of aggression; it was a challenge to the very notion of peace and security. It underscored the fragility of the status quo and the urgent need for solutions that addressed not just the symptoms of the conflict, but its root causes.

The refugee crisis spawned by the war remains unresolved, with millions of Palestinians still living in refugee camps or the diaspora, many clinging to the keys of homes they have never seen. The question of a Palestinian state remains unanswered, its people divided by internal conflict and the complexities of international diplomacy. Israel, meanwhile, has grown and prospered, yet lives in a state of perpetual vigilance, its existence challenged by neighbors and the unhealed wounds of the past.

This book, 'The Israeli-Palestinian War,' does not claim to have all the answers. Instead, it offers a lens through which to view the complexities of a struggle that spans generations. It delves deep into the history and the heartache, the politics and the pain that have shaped this land and its people.

As I sit here, penning these lines, I am acutely aware of the criticisms that may arise. Some may argue that focusing on Israeli suffering obscures the plight of Palestinian civilians caught in the crossfire. Others may contend that such accounts serve to justify or perpetuate the status quo. I believe acknowledging pain is not a zero-sum game. The anguish of one does not negate the suffering of another; rather, it calls us to a deeper empathy for all victims of this protracted struggle.

In drawing connections to the overarching themes of this book, it is imperative to recognize that the human cost of the invasion is not merely a footnote in the annals of history. It is a stark reminder of the urgent need for a sustainable and just resolution to a conflict that has claimed too many lives and fractured too many families.

In the heart of the conflict, a stark revelation pierces the consciousness of the international community: One in every three hostages taken during the Israeli-Palestinian war is under the age of eighteen. The implications of this statistic are profound, casting a shadow over the innocence of youth and thrusting the world into a moral quandary.

Such a fact is not merely a number, but a reflection of a grim reality that touches on the very essence of the conflict's brutality. It unveils the depth of the crisis - that the young, whose lives are yet to unfold, are captured in the unforgiving grip of war. This chilling truth stands as a testament to the urgency with which this conflict must be addressed, not only for the sake of present generations but for the future of the region itself.

As we witness the shattering of innocence, the unraveling of families, and the international community's scramble to respond, we must ask ourselves: How did we come to this, and where do we go from here? These are not idle questions but calls to action that demands contemplation, strategy, and, above all, a humanistic approach to conflict resolution.

Step by step, bridges the gap between shocking revelations and the pursuit of knowledge, guiding readers through the labyrinth of military engagements, diplomatic negotiations, and the tenacious fight for humanitarian justice. Beyond the mere statistics and news headlines, there lies a narrative of individuals, the hostages themselves, each with a name, a story, and a life interrupted by the tumult of war.

But what of the captors, those who wield the power to instill fear and dictate the fates of their hostages? Their identities, too, are dissected with precision, not to sensationalize, but to understand. It is within the minds of these individuals that the seeds of conflict find fertile ground.

As I weave this intricate tale, the narrative transcends the boundaries of traditional military historiography. It becomes a beacon for the lost and a voice for the voiceless, illuminating the plight of captives and capturing the essence of human resilience.

In a world often numb to the suffering of distant others, 'The Israeli-Palestinian War' serves as a stark reminder of our shared humanity. It is a call to remember that beyond the strategies and the geopolitics, there are lives hanging in the balance - lives that depend on the actions and decisions of those in power, as well as the collective will of the global populace.

In the shadowed corridors of history, where the echoes of past conflicts reverberate, the story of the Israeli-Palestinian struggle is not a solitary chapter, but rather a complex, interwoven series of events that have shaped the geopolitics of the modern age. This enduring struggle, embroidered with the threads of cultural, religious, and territorial disputes, has invited global attention and intervention for decades. To grasp the present, we must first traverse the halls of the past, where the seeds of contention were sown and have since germinated into the thorny issues of today.

Fast forward to the present, where the reverberations of these milestones are felt in every rocket launch, every diplomatic initiative, and every plea for peace. In the current milieu, the stakes are higher than ever, as the world grapples with the implications of a war that ensnares not just the region, but all who stand in solidarity or opposition to the warring factions.

As we pivot from the history of the past to the unfolding narrative of our book, a rich blend of international responses begins to emerge. Nations across the world, from the power corridors of Washington and the grand halls of the United Nations to the bustling markets of the Middle East and beyond, have all been drawn into the whirlpool of the Israeli-Palestinian conflict. The attack, a grim reminder of the fragility of peace, has obtained a symphony of voices some harmonious, others discordant in the global arena.

Consider, for a moment, the United States, a nation long seen as a staunch ally of Israel. How did the White House, nestled thousands of miles away from the smoldering ruins of conflict, react to the news of the attack? With a nuanced blend of support for Israel's right to self-defense and calls for restraint, the American response encapsulated the duality of a superpower's role on the world stage.

Across the Atlantic, European capitals buzzed with diplomatic fervor, crafting statements and resolutions that sought to balance the historic ties to Israel with a growing concern for Palestinian sovereignty and human rights. From London to Berlin, from Paris to Rome, the

Old World watched with bated breath, its leaders walking the tightrope of diplomacy with practiced caution.

But what of the Middle Eastern countries, those whose very sands were shaken by the tremors of the attack? The Arab world, once united in opposition to Israel's existence, now presented a mosaic of stances. Some nations, like Egypt and Jordan, which have signed peace treaties with Israel, called for de-escalation and dialogue, while others harbored a simmering resentment, a reminder of the demanding complexities of regional politics.

And within the hallowed assembly of the United Nations, a battle of narratives unfolded. Representatives from around the globe took the stage, each vying to sway the court of world opinion. Condemnations and calls for a ceasefire were interspersed with passionate pleas for justice and sovereignty. It was here, amidst the flags of many nations, that the world sought to find a façade of unity in its response to the crisis.

In the aftermath of the attack, the diplomatic gears churned with urgency, as envoys shuttled between capitals. Ceasefires were brokered and broken, and humanitarian aid was dispatched with fervent hope. The global political response was a testament to the interconnectedness of our world, where the reverberations of a single event can ripple across oceans and continents.

In the end, the world's reactions are but a mirror, reflecting the myriad faces of those who look upon the war-torn region with eyes wide open. It is our shared duty to gaze into this mirror, to confront the truths it reveals, and to act with the wisdom that only history can impart. Only then can we aspire to craft a world, where the specter of war gives way to the light of understanding and the promise of peace.

As you turn these pages, I invite you to join me on a journey of discovery. Let your curiosity lead you through the narratives of those who have lived the conflict, whose lives have been elevated by the tactics of power and the pursuit of peace. Allow your imagination to be stirred by their stories, told with the authenticity of someone who has walked the corridors of power and the alleys of refugee camps alike.

I leave you with a question that has haunted me throughout the writing of this book: How might the resilience and unity displayed by civilians under fire inform our pursuit of peace? Could the very attributes that have enabled survival in times of war become the building blocks for reconciliation in times of peace?

The answer, I believe, lies not in the realm of rhetoric, but in the realm of possibility, a possibility that is born from the indomitable human spirit. It is this spirit that must guide us as we continue to navigate the complex landscape of the Israeli-Palestinian War, seeking pathways to a future where the sirens of war fall silent and the whispers of hope grow loud.

In today's context, the echoes of these ideologies are heard in the ongoing debate over a two-state solution, the right of return for Palestinian refugees, and the status of Jerusalem. The emotion and rhetoric may have evolved, but the fundamental issues at heart remain unchanged.

The 7th of October 2023 will be remembered as a day when the veneer of a tenuous peace was violently stripped away, unveiling the stark reality of a region in turmoil. As the sun rose that morning, it did not illuminate a path toward reconciliation, but cast light on a landscape that had been fundamentally altered. The barrage of rockets and the cries of the wounded became the indication of a new chapter in an old saga. And so, we stand at the cliff, peering into the unknown that awaits us. What lessons will we draw from the ashes of this latest conflagration? How will the stories of those lost and those still fighting for their place in the world shape the future of this ancient land?

Beneath the surface of what the headlines portray lies a fabric woven with the lives of millions, each thread a story of hopes, dreams, and oftentimes, unspeakable tragedy. This book seeks not only to chronicle the events that have led us to the present dead-end but also to understand the human cost of a land divided. This is not a book of despair; it is a manifesto of hope, a call to action for those who believe in the power of empathy to transcend borders and barriers.

My unique perspective, forged in my diverse experiences from the discipline of the military to the innovation of the corporate world, from the nurturing halls of education to the fertile grounds of social entrepreneurship provides a multifaceted lens through which to view this conflict. I approach this not just as a chronicler of facts, but as an empathetic participant in the human struggle for dignity and peace. Together, we can chart a course toward a future where the olive trees stand as symbols of peace, not as silent protectors of sorrow.

Do the lines drawn in the sand, carving out nations from the vast Middle Eastern desert, tell the full story of these people's disagreement? We must probe deeper, beyond the surface of maps and mandates.

TABLE OF CONTENTS

Chapter 1

THE UNENDING SAGA OF THE ISRAELI-PALESTINIAN CONFLICT

*I*n the twilight of the Ottoman Empire, as the Great War's shadow loomed large, the world's powers congregated, carving up spheres of influence with lines that would shape the destiny of nations. The globe is agitated by the suffering of war, empires are insecure and on the brink of dissolution, and a declaration penned in the quiet corridors of power in London is poised to ignite a century of contention.

Throughout the years of British administration, waves of Jewish immigrants arrived, fleeing persecution and dreaming of a new life in their ancestral land. Simultaneously, Arab nationalism was on the rise, with the indigenous population increasingly viewing the growing Jewish presence as a direct threat to their own national aspirations. Tensions simmered, periodically boiling over into violent confrontations, as both Jews and Arabs felt betrayed by British policies that seemed to favor one side, then the other.

The Great Migration

In the dynamic and often deafening history of the Middle East, the phenomenon of Jewish immigration to Palestine stands out as a pivotal element in shaping the modern Israeli-Palestinian conflict. 'The Great Migration,' delves into the intricacies of this demographic transformation, tracing the journey of Jewish immigrants, who sought sanctuary and a new beginning in the ancestral lands of their ancestors.

It all began with the stirrings of national consciousness and the rapidly growing Zionist movement in the late 19th century. As waves of mass murder swept across Eastern Europe, many Jews looked towards Palestine as a beacon of hope, a place to reclaim a sense of belonging and establish a secure homeland. This quest was inspired by both spiritual emotion and the clear necessity of finding refuge from persecution.

The earliest origins of this migration can be linked to the First Aliyah, which occurred between 1882 and 1903. Inspired by pioneers who sought to revitalize the Jewish connection to the land, small groups began to settle in Palestine, purchasing plots to cultivate the soil and lay the foundations of future communities. These early settlers faced immense hardships, from disease to difficulties in adjusting to a new agrarian lifestyle, yet they persevered, driven by their vision.

As we chronicle this journey, the Second Aliyah (1904-1914), marked by socialist ideologies, brought about the establishment of the community movement, and collective farms that became the backbone of agricultural development in the region.

Cultural and regional variations were evident, as the Jewish population in Palestine became more diverse. The Third (1919-1923) and Fourth Aliyah's (1924-1929) saw Jews from different parts of Europe and Yemen contribute their unique traditions and customs, enriching the cultural landscape. These immigrants brought with them skills in trade and crafts, bolstering the urban growth alongside rural settlements.

However, as the Jewish population grew, so did tensions with the Arab inhabitants of Palestine. Land ownership disputes became increasingly common, as did clashes over access to resources. The British Mandate for Palestine, established in 1920, attempted to manage these competing national aspirations but often aggravated them.

The Fifth Aliyah (1929-1939) was particularly significant, as it coincided with the rise of Nazi Germany and an urgent need for a safe haven for Jews. The influx of tens of thousands of Jewish refugees during this period intensified the demographic shift, resulting in heightened conflict over the land and its future.

Have you ever wondered how the echoes of these distant footsteps still reverberate through the hills and valleys of the Holy Land? How the hopes and dreams of those early immigrants have shaped the region's destiny?

The Holocaust and the horrors of World War II brought about a turning point in the narrative of Jewish immigration. The desperation of survivors seeking refuge and the international community's response profoundly influenced the establishment of the State of Israel in 1948. This event marked both a culmination of the Zionist dream and a moment of profound loss and displacement for the Palestinian Arabs.

In discussing modern interpretations, we must acknowledge the ongoing debate around the right of return for Palestinian refugees and the question of Jewish settlements in the West Bank. These issues remain at the heart of the conflict, with demographic concerns still central to both Israeli and Palestinian narratives.

Challenges and controversies continue to increase, as both sides grapple with the legacy of the past and the implications for the future. The issue of land ownership, the right to self-determination, and the quest for peace are as relevant now, as they were a century ago.

The Great Migration is not merely a historical phenomenon, but a thread that weaves through the fabric of current affairs in the Middle East. As we reflect on the path walked by so many, we find ourselves at a crossroads, searching for a way to move forward together, despite the weight of history. Can the lessons of the past illuminate the road to a shared future? Can we find a way to honor the memories of those who journeyed so far, with the hope of living side by side in peace?

As the pages of history turn, 'The Great Migration' remains a testament to the enduring human spirit, to the resilience of those who dared to dream of a better life in the land of their ancestors, and to the complex collage of land that continues to be the ordeal of national aspirations and the quest for peace.

Partition and War

In the shadow of a world recovering from the ravages of the Second World War, the year 1947 heralded a pivotal moment in the history of the Middle East. The land of Palestine, ancient and venerated, stood at the cusp of monumental change. Whispers of a United Nations resolution that sought to partition the land into two separate states, one Jewish, and one Arab, were stirring the winds of conflict and hope alike. This was a kingdom where centuries of co-existence were about to be challenged by the aspirations of two peoples, each yearning for a nation to call their own.

As the sun set on November 29, 1947, the UN General Assembly adopted Resolution 181, endorsing the partition plan. The Jewish community in Palestine, represented by the Jewish Agency, accepted the plan with jubilation, seeing it as the long-awaited legitimization of their aspirations. Conversely, the Arab inhabitants and their leadership, perceiving the decision as a betrayal of their rights, rejected it vehemently. The landscape was now set for confrontation; the die had been cast, and the echoes of celebration mingled with the murmurs of brewing discontent.

Could it be that history was always destined to lead us here, to this moment, where two divergent paths collided? The UN's partition plan, idealistic in its intent, failed to reconcile the complex realities on the ground. The months that followed saw a spiraling descent into violence, with skirmishes and reprisals escalating into full-blown warfare. The British, their mandate expiring, were eager to wash their hands of the conflict, leaving a vacuum that would soon be filled by the clamor of war.

The shadow of 1948 looms large in the collective memory of the region. It was in this year that the State of Israel declared its independence, a declaration that was met with immediate armed conflict, as neighboring Arab states launched an invasion. The ensuing 1947-1949 Palestine War, also known as the War of Independence or the Nakba, depending on one's perspective, reshaped the geography and demography of the land. Battles raged, villages were lost, and hundreds of thousands of Palestinian Arabs found themselves refugees. For Jews, the war was a struggle for survival and sovereignty; for Arabs, it was a catastrophe that fractured their society and homeland.

And what of the consequences of that war which we still grapple with today? The peace agreements of 1949 drew new lines, both physical and metaphorical, carving out a West Bank under Jordanian control and a Gaza Strip governed by Egypt. Jerusalem was left divided, its eastern part annexed by Jordan, while the west became part of the nascent Israeli state. These borders, intended as temporary, became a de facto reality, setting the stage for the enduring conflict that has continued to define the region.

In understanding the present, we must acknowledge the shadows of the past. The refugee crisis spawned by the war remains unresolved, with millions of Palestinians still living in refugee camps or the diaspora, many clinging to the keys of homes they have never seen. The question of a Palestinian state remains unanswered, its people divided by internal conflict and the complexities of international diplomacy. Israel, meanwhile, has grown and prospered, yet lives in a state of perpetual vigilance, its existence challenged by neighbors and the unhealed wounds of the past.

Why does history matter now, in a world where the urgency of the present often overshadows the lessons of yesteryear? The answer is simple: Because without understanding the origins of the conflict, without recognizing the grievances and aspirations of both Israelis and Palestinians, the path to peace remains shrouded in the mists of misunderstanding.

Let us then, with the full weight of history upon our shoulders, transition from the historical overview into the exploration of how the 1947-1949 Palestine War shaped the landscape of today's conflicts. As the narrative unfolds in the pages to follow, we will delve deep into the heart of the matter, seeking to uncover the truths that might lead us toward reconciliation and coexistence. With each step, the hope is to illuminate the present through the prism of the past, ever mindful of the human stories etched into the land, a land that has seen empires rise and fall, yet remains the enduring testament to the resilience of its people.

As the contours of history take shape before us, remember this: The path to peace is often a journey through the corridors of time, where understanding the partition and war of yesteryear might just pave the way for harmony tomorrow.

Sectarian Conflict

Amidst the hustle of marketplaces and the whisper of ancient olive trees, the land that would come to be the stage for the Israeli-Palestinian conflict was no stranger to the intermingling of cultures and religions. Here, Jews, Christians, and Muslims had lived side by side, their histories entangled within the complex alleys of Jerusalem, the fertile fields of Galilee, and the desert region of the turmoil. Yet, beneath this veneer of coexistence, tensions simmered, stoked by nationalist sentiments and geopolitical maneuvering.

The central figures in this unfolding drama were the Arab and Jewish communities of Palestine. The Jews, rejuvenated by the Zionist movement, sought to re-establish their ancestral homeland, while the Arabs, the majority population, resisted what they perceived as encroachment upon their land and rights. This dichotomy set the stage for the core challenge at the heart of the case study: the escalating conflict between these two nationalistic movements, each fuelled by a powerful mix of history, religion, and a profound sense of belonging to the land.

As the British Mandate waned, the strategies employed by each side grew increasingly polarized. The Jewish community, under the leadership of figures like David Ben-Gurion, organized themselves politically and militarily, forming the Haganah (underground Jewish militia), the precursor to the Israel Defense Forces. In contrast, the Arab community, though lacking a unified command, carried out a series of uprisings and boycotts, attempting to thwart the Zionist enterprise.

The results of these early confrontations were mixed. Jewish settlements expanded, strengthened by a well-organized structure and support from the international Jewish diaspora. Conversely, the Arab community experienced fragmentation, with local and family loyalties often superseding broader nationalist goals. This disunity, coupled with a lack of substantial international backing, left the Arab community at a disadvantage.

Reflecting upon these early years of conflict, one cannot help but ponder the multitude of 'what ifs.' What if the Arab leadership had united early on, presenting a cohesive front against the partition? What if the international community had engaged more robustly to mediate the dispute? The answers to these questions remain speculative, but they underscore the critical role of leadership and international involvement, or lack thereof, in shaping the course of events.

This manifestation of sectarian conflict is but one thread in the larger narrative of the Israeli-Palestinian War. It reveals patterns of behavior and decision-making that resonate throughout the subsequent decades of conflict. The early years of violence and discord set precedents and established mindsets that have proven difficult to dislodge, forming a legacy of suspicion and reactive policies.

We shall traverse further into the intricate maze of the Israeli-Palestinian War, exploring pivotal events and dissecting the decisions that have led us to the present deadlock. With each step, we uncover layers of complexity, and with each revelation, we gain insights into the enduring human quest for dignity, security, and a place to call home.

The Suez Canal Crisis and Pan-Arabism

At the dawn of the 20th century, the Ottoman Empire's grip on the Middle East began to wane, setting the stage for new powers to assert their influence over the region. The earliest origins of the Suez Crisis can be traced back to the strategic importance of the Suez Canal, a vital artery for maritime trade connecting the Mediterranean Sea to the Red Sea. Who would control this valuable waterway was a question that simmered below the surface of international relations.

In the fabric of Middle Eastern history, the threads of conflict and cooperation are intricately woven, creating a pattern that resonates with the echoes of ancient struggles and modern aspirations. In the shadow of the 1948 Arab-Israeli War, the Middle East remained a region simmering with unresolved tensions and competing national interests. One pivotal event that would further shape the geopolitics of the area was the Suez Crisis of 1956, a confrontation involving Egypt, Israel, Britain, and France, which would inadvertently serve as a catalyst for a broader Arab unity against what was perceived as Western imperialism and aggression.

Historically, the Suez Canal's roots date back to 1869, when it was opened after ten years of construction, financed by European investors, and built using Egyptian labor. It was a marvel of engineering, but also an example of European intervention in the Middle East. Nasser's nationalization reversed this historical power dynamic.

The term 'Suez Crisis' refers to a diplomatic and military conflict, precipitated by Egyptian President, Gamal Abdel Nasser's nationalization of the Suez Canal. This strategic waterway, long under British control, was the lifeline for maritime trade, particularly Europe's access to Asian and Middle Eastern oil. Nasser's bold move was both a declaration of sovereignty and an assertion of non-alignment in the Cold War context.

The first significant milestone, in the path to the Suez Crisis, occurred in the aftermath of World War II. The decline of British and French colonial power and the rise of nationalist movements across the Arab world catalyzed a shift in regional dynamics. Egypt, under the leadership of President Gamal Abdel Nasser, became the standard-bearer of Arab nationalism. Nasser's vision of pan-Arab unity and socialism posed a direct challenge to Western interests in the Middle East.

Does history not teach us that the desire for autonomy often leads nations to dramatic confrontations? It was Nasser's nationalization of the Suez Canal in 1956 that lit the fuse of the crisis. This audacious move was a declaration of Egypt's sovereignty over its resources, a rejection of neo-colonial influence, and it sent shockwaves through the capitals of London, Paris, and beyond.

The response was swift and coordinated. Israel, Britain, and France hatched a secret plan to regain control of the canal and remove Nasser from power. The Israeli army launched a surprise attack on the Sinai Peninsula, quickly advancing toward the canal. Britain and France, under the guise of protecting international interests, issued an ultimatum and then intervened militarily. The world watched, aghast, as a new chapter of conflict unfolded.

Through whispers of diplomatic cables and the sharp images of tanks rolling across deserts, the Suez Crisis was etched into public consciousness. Soldiers entrenched in the sand, ships blockaded in the canal, and civilians caught in the crossfire.

The cultural and regional variations in response to the crisis were profound. While the Western powers sought to maintain their waning influence, the United States, wary of Soviet expansion and the principles of self-determination, hesitated to support the tripartite invasion. Meanwhile, the Soviet Union saw an opportunity to extend its reach by supporting Egypt. The Arab world, though not monolithic, largely rallied behind Nasser as a hero resisting imperialism.

In the modern interpretations of the Suez Crisis, it is seen as a watershed moment when the United States and the Soviet Union began to exert more direct influence over the Middle East, signaling the decline of the old European colonial powers. The crisis also had significant implications for the Israeli-Palestinian conflict, as it strengthened Israel and confirmed its military capability, while also highlighting the limitations of Arab unity.

The challenges and controversies of the Suez Crisis were manifold, but perhaps the most significant turning point came with the intervention of the United Nations. International pressure, especially from the United States, forced Britain, France, and Israel to withdraw their forces. This marked the first time that a major international crisis was defused through diplomacy led by a global organization, setting a precedent for future peacekeeping operations.

The legacy of the Suez Crisis is complex and multifaceted. It was a humbling episode for Britain and France, accelerated the process of decolonization, and supported the strategic importance of the Middle East in global politics. For Israel, it was a demonstration of military capability that would influence its future dealings with neighboring Arab states.

The echoes of the Suez Crisis are still felt today. As we examine the shifting sands of Middle Eastern geopolitics, we must ask ourselves: What can we learn from the interplay of nationalism and international diplomacy that characterized this period? How might the principles of sovereignty and the lessons of history guide us in resolving contemporary conflicts?

Six-Day War and Occupation in 1967

The shadow of the Suez Crisis had barely receded when the Middle East found itself at the height of yet another conflict, one that would redefine the region's geopolitical contours. The year 1967 heralded the advent of the Six-Day War, a conflict belied by its enduring consequences, particularly the occupation of Palestinian territories by Israel. We will dissect this pivotal event and the protracted aftermath that reshaped the Israeli-Palestinian narrative.

From the residue of the 1956 conflict, tensions simmered, stoked by a confluence of nationalistic emotion, territorial disputes, and the superpowers' strategic gamesmanship. The inception point can be traced to the immediate post-Suez period, where a relative calm contradict the underlying conflict. The Arab nations, though chastened by the outcome of the Suez Crisis, still nursed aspirations to assert their sovereignty and resist Israeli expansion.

As the 1960s unfolded, a series of provocations and reprisals became the norm. Skirmishes along border areas, particularly with Syria over the Golan Heights, and increased guerrilla activities by Palestinian factions against Israel, escalated tensions. A major milestone in the chronology of conflict was the formation of the Palestine Liberation Organization (PLO) in 1964, which sought to unite various Palestinian groups and intensify their struggle.

How did the world react to the growing friction and the threat of war? The international community remained largely on edge, with the Cold War's superpowers viewing the Middle East as a chessboard for their grand geopolitical strategies. Arab nations, though united in their opposition to Israel, often harbored divergent strategies and ambitions. The charismatic Egyptian President, Gamal Abdel Nasser, whose actions had catalyzed the Suez Crisis, continued to be a figurehead of Arab nationalism and resistance against Israel.

June 5, 1967, marked the explosive beginning of the Six-Day War. Israel, feeling increasingly encircled by Arab armies and the closure of the Straits of Tiran, launched pre-emptive airstrikes, decimating the air forces of Egypt, Jordan, and Syria. What followed was a rapid succession of Israeli ground operations that stunned the world with their effectiveness. Within days, Israel had captured the Gaza Strip and the Sinai Peninsula from Egypt, the West Bank from Jordan, and the Golan Heights from Syria.

The resulting occupation signaled a new phase in the Israeli-Palestinian conflict. Israeli sovereignty extended over a large Palestinian population and holy sites, aggravating the struggle for national identity and autonomy. Modern interpretations of the Six-Day War and the subsequent occupation vary greatly. For some, it represents a miraculous victory for Israel, a testament to its military brilliance and survival instinct. For others, particularly Palestinians and their supporters, it marks the beginning of a painful era of displacement and subjugation.

Recent developments have seen attempts at peace negotiations, interspersed with bouts of violence and uprisings. The Oslo Accords of the 1990s brought hope for a two-state solution, but the roadmap to peace has been fraught with obstacles and setbacks. The question lingers in the air, heavy and unresolved: Is a lasting peace achievable in a land so deeply scarred by war and occupation?

The challenges, controversies, and turning points of this period are numerous. The 1973, Yom Kippur War, the revolt and the ongoing settlement activities in the occupied territories have all added layers of complexity to the conflict. Each event has left an enduring mark on the collective memory of the region's inhabitants, shaping their narratives and their claims to the land.

Fast forward to the present day, and the reverberations of the British Mandate are still visibly felt. Its legacy is etched in the checkpoints and separation barriers, in the UN resolutions and peace accords, in the very fabric of daily life for Israelis and Palestinians alike. The Mandate's expiration in 1948 and the subsequent declaration of the State of Israel marked another watershed moment, one that would lead to war, disruption, and an ongoing struggle for self-determination. The past is prologue, and the narrative threads woven by the British Mandate continue to entangle all efforts towards a resolution.

The story of the Israeli-Palestinian conflict is far from over and is but one chapter in a saga that continues to unfold. As you delve deeper into this book, I invite you to reflect on the power of history, not as a relic of the past, but as a living force that shapes our present and our future.

Peace, elusive and fragile, remains the ultimate goal, a beacon of hope in a region, too often engulfed in the shadows of war. As we journey through these pages, let us keep our eyes trained on that horizon, however distant it might seem. In the words of the poet, "We must accept finite disappointment, but never lose infinite hope."

Chapter 2

GENESIS OF CONFLICT- THE BALFOUR DECLARATION

*I*n the dimming light of a 1917 November evening, British Foreign Secretary, Arthur James Balfour, penned a letter that would ripple through the records of history, sowing seeds of contention and hope in equal measure. This document, known simply as the Balfour Declaration, would come to symbolize both a promise and a plight, a beacon of safety for Jews and a spirit of displacement for Arabs. But to understand the magnitude of this letter's influence, a journey through the complex of historical events that shaped its creation is essential.

Europe was shaken under the strain of the First World War, an epoch of bloodshed that re-drew borders and re-defined power balances. Across the Ottoman Empire, the winds of change were blowing, as Arab nationalism began to stir under the yoke of their rulers. Simultaneously, the Zionist movement, fuelled by centuries of persecution and the dream of self-determination, was gaining momentum. These were the historical milestones, intersecting at a crossroad, that led to the promise of a Jewish homeland in Palestine.

In the ignited aftermath of war, empires crumbled, and nations rose from their ashes. The Ottoman

Empire's collapse left the future of its Arab territories, including Palestine, covered in uncertainty. The Sykes-Picot Agreement, a secret pact between Britain and France, had already carved up the Middle East into spheres of influence, disregarding the aspirations of its inhabitants. Yet, history's pendulum swung again with the Balfour Declaration, a mere sixty-seven words that pledged British support for the establishment of a 'national home for the Jewish people' in Palestine, with the caveat that, "Nothing shall be done which may prejudice the civil and religious rights of existing non-Jewish communities."

The declaration's ambiguity sowed discord from the onset. While Jews across the world rejoiced at the prospect of a sanctuary after millennia of diaspora, the Arab population of Palestine felt a deep sense of betrayal. They saw in the declaration the specter of colonial dispossession, fearing the erosion of their own nationalist aspirations.

But how could such a promise be kept in a land already inhabited by a majority Arab population? Did the architects of this document foresee the enduring conflict their words would engender?

As the ink dried on the Balfour Declaration, it sowed the seeds of hope for Zionists craving for a homeland, while simultaneously laying the groundwork for a growing sense of unease among the Arab inhabitants of Palestine. In this delicate dance of diplomacy and imperial interests, the stage was set for a clash of national aspirations that would outlast the British Empire's own lifespan.

Following the war's end, the League of Nations entrusted

Britain with the Mandate for Palestine, legitimizing British governance and the implementation of the Balfour Declaration's intent. With the stroke of a pen, the Mandate formalized the British role in shaping the region's future, but at what cost to those who called Palestine their home?

What does it mean to transplant one people's hope onto another's ancestral soil? Can the longing for a homeland justify the displacement of another? These questions, as relevant today as they were a century ago, lie at the heart of the Israeli-Palestinian conflict.

The declaration's centennial has passed, yet its implications penetrate every facet of Israeli and Palestinian life. It is a stark reminder that history's edicts are not merely words on paper; they are the foundations upon which nations are built and identities are forged.

As the story unfolds, we delve deeper into the intricacies of the British government's promise, and its lasting impact on Arab nationalism. The declaration, intended as a wartime strategy to rally Jewish support, became a cornerstone of the Middle East's geopolitical landscape. Amid the debates and discussions, one must not forget the lives entangled in its legacy lives, marked by struggle and yearning, loss and resilience.

The Balfour Declaration stands not only as a historical milestone but also as a symbol of the enduring quest for a place to call home. It is a narrative woven into the fabric of a land sacred to many, a land that continues to be both a haven and a battleground.

The narrative now pivots to the contemporary exploration your book undertakes. What lessons can be obtained from the interweaving of Jewish dreams and Arab disillusionment? How can the past inform a future where coexistence is not a mere aspiration, but a tangible reality? As we traverse the complex terrain of the Israeli-Palestinian conflict, the Balfour Declaration serves as a sad starting point, a chapter in history that begs reflection and, perhaps, can light the path toward reconciliation.

The echoes of the Balfour Declaration still resound in the clamor of the Israeli-Palestinian conflict. The century-old document is a historical lodestone for understanding the current impasse, a testament to the enduring influence of past promises on present realities. The question lingers: How can the wounds of history be healed when its legacy casts such a long shadow?

The UN Partition Plan and Its Aftermath

As dawn broke over the land of Palestine, the year 1947 brought with it winds of change that would soon escalate into a tempest. With the end of the British Mandate on the horizon, the United Nations stepped forward with a controversial solution that would attempt to untangle the knot of Jewish and Arab national aspirations, a partition plan that would divide the land into two separate states.

The Holocaust had dramatically underscored the plight of Europe's Jews, intensifying international support for a Jewish state. Meanwhile, the Arabs of Palestine, bolstered by the emerging Arab nationalism across the Middle East, vehemently opposed any plan that would compromise their claim to the land.

The UN Partition Plan of 1947 aimed to carve out an

independent Jewish state and an independent Arab state, with Jerusalem under international control. It was a proposal fraught with complexity and destined to sow the seeds of further discord. The Jewish community, though not fully satisfied with the territorial division, largely accepted the plan; it was a pragmatic step toward realizing their long-held dream of statehood. The Arab community, however, rejected the plan outright, viewing it as an unjust partition of their homeland and a violation of their right to self-determination.

The rejection of the partition plan by the Arab states and Palestinian Arabs set the stage for the 1948 Arab-Israeli War, known in Israel as the War of Independence and to Palestinians as the Nakba, or catastrophe. The fighting commenced with sporadic clashes but quickly escalated into a full-scale conflict with the expiration of the British Mandate and the declaration of the State of Israel on May 14, 1948.

The war's aftermath was profound and far-reaching. By its end, Israel had expanded its territory beyond the original UN proposal, and hundreds of thousands of Palestinian Arabs had fled or been expelled from their homes, creating a refugee crisis that remains unresolved to this day. The Arab states, having failed to prevent the establishment of Israel, found themselves grappling with a humbling defeat and the reality of a new neighbor.

Instead of resorting to conflict, the parties could have returned to the negotiating table. Perhaps an international peacekeeping force could have been established to maintain order, while a more gradual approach to independence and state-building was undertaken. Such a strategy might have involved a federated or confederated model, with autonomous

Jewish and Arab areas linked by a central government tasked with ensuring equitable resource distribution and the protection of minority rights.

The implementation of such a solution would have required visionary leadership and immense international support. It would have necessitated concessions from both sides, a willingness to compromise for the greater good. Evidence from other conflicts suggests that peacekeeping and power-sharing arrangements can reduce violence, and provide a framework for more stable governance. In the case of the Israeli-Palestinian conflict, it could have perhaps mitigated the mass displacement and ensuing animosity that has characterized the struggle.

As we reflect on the partition plan and its tumultuous aftermath, we must ask ourselves, what can be learned from this chapter of history? How can we apply the lessons of the past to avoid the repetition of such tragedies? In the search for peace, we must never underestimate the power of dialogue and the importance of mutual respect and understanding. It is only through the acknowledgment of each other's narratives and the willingness to forge a shared future that a lasting solution to the Israeli-Palestinian conflict can be found.

It is this understanding that compels us to look beyond the battlefields and borders, to the hearts and minds of those who call this land home. Their stories, their dreams, and their unyielding spirit are the true heartbeat of history. And it is in their collective yearning for peace that we find the most profound call to action, a call that echoes through the decades, urging us to envision a horizon where the sun sets, not on conflict, but on a landscape of reconciliation and hope.

The Territorial Shifts

In the wake of the Suez Crisis, the Middle East was left teetering on a precarious balance of power. The region, steeped in ancient history, found itself at the crossroads of a modern struggle for land and identity. This volatile backdrop set the stage for one of the most definitive conflicts in the 20th century: the 1967, Six-Day War. This brief confrontation dramatically altered the map of the Middle East, embedding itself as a pivotal moment in the Israeli-Palestinian discourse.

The national aspirations and fears, coupled with the religious significance of the land, fuelled a climate of mutual distrust and animosity. The ceasefire lines of 1949, which marked the end of hostilities, were never recognized as official borders by the Arab states, leaving Israel surrounded by neighbors who questioned its very existence.

As the years passed, tensions simmered. A series of skirmishes, border disputes, and political maneuvers characterized the relationship between Israel and its Arab neighbors. A crucial milestone occurred in November 1966, when an Israeli retaliatory raid into the Jordanian-controlled West Bank village of Samu escalated tensions. This event prompted a realignment of Arab forces, with Egypt, Jordan, and Syria growing increasingly cooperative against what they perceived as the common Israeli threat.

The war itself was a whirlwind of military precision and surprise. On June 5, 1967, Israel launched a pre-emptive strike against Egypt, destroying much of its air force on the ground. Within hours, Israeli forces engaged Jordanian and Syrian armies, seizing control of Jerusalem's Old City, the West Bank, the Gaza Strip, the Sinai Peninsula, and the Golan Heights, all within six days. The Golan Heights, overlooking the Israeli Hula Valley, previously a Syrian artillery position menacing Israeli communities below, now stood under Israeli control. Jerusalem, a city torn in two since 1948, was reunified under Israeli authority, stirring profound emotions on all sides.

Cultural and regional variations played a significant role in the war's progression and aftermath. Israel, with a predominantly Jewish population, viewed the reunification of Jerusalem as a historic and religious triumph. In contrast, Palestinians and the larger Arab world saw the loss of territories as a devastating blow to their national aspirations and territorial integrity.

For Israelis, the war is often seen as a necessary act of self-defense that resulted in a reunified Jerusalem and defensible borders. For Palestinians and many Arab citizens, the war marked the beginning of an ongoing occupation, with the West Bank and Gaza Strip becoming focal points for Palestinian statehood ambitions.

The war also marked a significant turning point, with the United Nations Security Council Resolution 242 calling for the 'withdrawal of Israeli armed forces from territories occupied in the recent conflict' and acknowledgment that 'every state in the area... live in peace, within secure and recognized boundaries, free from threats or acts of force.' This resolution remains a cornerstone for peace negotiations to this day.

The war's outcome and the continued Israeli presence in the territories have been central to the Israeli-Palestinian conflict and broader Arab-Israeli relations. The question of land for peace, the status of Jerusalem, and the right of return for Palestinian refugees are issues that have echoed through the decades, fuelling cycles of negotiation and conflict.

In sum, the Six-Day War was not merely a clash of armies; it was a transformational event that reshaped the geopolitical contours of the Middle East. Its reverberations are felt to this day, as the struggle for land, identity, and peace continues to define the Israeli-Palestinian narrative. As we look back on this chapter of history, we see a mosaic of courage, fear, hope, and despair, a sad reminder of how swiftly the tides of war can redraw the lines that define nations and their peoples.

Uprising and the Oslo Accords

In the wake of the Six-Day War's profound alterations, the Israeli-Palestinian landscape was indelibly changed, setting the stage for further conflict and attempts at reconciliation. The oscillation between hope and despair in this noisy region is captured in the epochs of the uprising and the Oslo Accords, pivotal moments that underscore the complexity and depth of the Israeli-Palestinian conundrum.

The first Palestinian Intifada, or uprising, erupted in 1987, a spontaneous combustion of decades-long frustrations. It was a grassroots movement characterized by stone-throwing youths confronting a well-armed military. Scenes of such David versus Goliath encounters seared into global consciousness, eliciting both sympathy and condemnation. The uprising brought forward the harsh realities of occupation into the living rooms of the world, making the Palestinian plight more visible and urgent than ever before.

The claim here is clear: The uprising was a crucial turning point, a manifestation of Palestinian national identity, and a catalyst for political change. Concrete evidence supporting this claim lies in the material and social impacts of the uprising. The Palestinian economy, heavily integrated with Israel's, suffered greatly due to widespread strikes and boycotts. Yet, the societal fabric of the Palestinians was strengthened, with local committees forming to manage education, health, and social services amid the chaos.

Delving deeper, the uprising reshaped the Palestinian political landscape. The Palestine Liberation Organization (PLO), led by Yasser Arafat, gained significant legitimacy as the representative of the Palestinian people during this period. The images of resilience and resistance resonated with the Palestinian diaspora and the broader Arab world, altering perceptions and strategies regarding the Israeli-Palestinian conflict.

However, counter-evidence suggests that the uprising also led to increased Israeli security measures and a hardening of attitudes among some Israelis, who saw the uprising as a threat to their safety. Settlement expansion in the occupied territories accelerated, further complicating the prospects for peace.

In rebuttal, the uprising did indeed provoke a tough security response, but it also led to increased international pressure for a peaceful resolution to the conflict. This intensified scrutiny laid the groundwork for the Oslo peace process. The secret negotiations that took place in Norway culminated in the Oslo Accords, an agreement aimed at fulfilling the right of the Palestinian people to self-determination.

The Oslo Accords represented a landmark moment, a glimmer of hope in a narrative often darkened by despair. The agreement established the Palestinian Authority and set a timeline for the withdrawal of Israeli forces from parts of the Gaza Strip and West Bank. It also laid the foundation for further negotiations on permanent status issues such as borders, refugees, settlements, security, and the status of Jerusalem.

Additional supporting evidence for the significance of the Oslo Accords comes from the iconic handshake between Yasser Arafat and Israeli Prime Minister Yitzhak Rabin on the White House lawn in 1993. This moment was emblematic of the potential for a historic reconciliation between two peoples long mired in conflict. It was a testament to the power of dialogue and the possibility of forging a new reality through compromise and understanding.

Yet, the path of Oslo was fraught with obstacles. The assassination of Yitzhak Rabin by a Jewish extremist in 1995 highlighted the deep divisions within Israeli society. Moreover, the persistent attacks by Palestinian militants against Israeli civilians during this period served to undermine the peace process and trust between the parties.

The conclusion that can be drawn from this period is that the uprising and the Oslo Accords were both critical in shaping the Israeli-Palestinian landscape. The uprising illustrated the consequences of prolonged occupation and the determination of the Palestinian people to seek self-determination. The Oslo Accords, despite their shortcomings and the ultimate derailment of the peace process, demonstrated that negotiation and mutual recognition could pave the way toward a resolution of the conflict.

Just to summarise, the story of the uprising and the Oslo Accords is one of fluctuating hope and despair. It is a narrative that reflects the enduring human yearning for freedom and peace, set against the backdrop of complex historical grievances and geopolitical realities. As the records of history continue to unfold, these periods remind us of the fragility of peace and the enduring necessity of striving for a just and lasting resolution to the Israeli-Palestinian conflict.

Chapter 3

THE OCTOBER 2023 SURPRISE-THE PRELUDE TO INVASION

In the dimming light of dusk, the ancient olive groves of the east bore silent witness to the growing unrest, a prelude to the cacophony of war that would soon shake the very foundations of the region. Here, where the roots of history burrow deep into the arid soil, the story of the Israeli-Palestinian conflict unfolds, a narrative woven with the threads of ancient enmities and modern political conspiracies.

The land, sacred to many, has been a crucible of civilization, a battleground for empires, and a fabric of cultures for millennia. A journey back through the corridors of time brings us to the birthplace of the three great monotheistic religions, Judaism, Christianity, and Islam, each laying claim to this sliver of earth, a claim that has sparked countless conflicts and shaped the destinies of nations.

The Gaza Strip, a land mired in poverty and conflict, has become synonymous with the struggle for Palestinian statehood and the resilience of people under siege. The surprise attack by Hamas-led forces, a meticulously planned operation that caught Israel off guard, an opening salvo that would once again plunge the region into turmoil. But what were the warning signs missed? What intelligence was ignored or misinterpreted?

As the sun set on an unremarkable day, the hum of everyday life in the bustling markets of Gaza and the quiet routines of Israeli border communities masked the clandestine movements and whispered orders that heralded the coming storm. In the shadows, militants prepared, weapons were smuggled, and tunnels, those harrowing arteries beneath the earth, bristled with the anticipation of conflict.

In the chambers of power and the back alleys of espionage, intelligence ticked away like a time bomb. Reports of unusual activity, intercepted communications, and the silent ballet of drones overhead, were all pieces of a puzzle that, when assembled, would reveal the mosaic of impending war. Yet, as so often in history, the clarity of hindsight was absent in the fog of the present.

As we delve deeper into the events that precipitated the attack, we encounter a blend of human endeavor and error. We meet individuals driven by duty and those consumed by vengeance. We see the interplay of geopolitics and the raw emotion of those living on the front lines. We explore the psyche of a region where the drumbeat of war is never too distant, and the yearning for peace is a fragile dream.

The stage is set, the actors are in motion and the world holds its breath, watching as the hustle once again becomes the arena for a confrontation, that reverberates far beyond its ancient hills and troubled shores. The introduction to invasion is not merely a recounting of events; it is an examination of the human spirit in the face of adversity, a reflection on the cost of conflict, and a meditation on the elusive nature of peace.

Rockets Over Israel

The night sky over Tel Aviv was ablaze with a constellation of destruction. Families who, moments earlier, were tucking their children into bed were now jolted awake, their hearts racing as the sirens wailed a chorus of impending doom. Each rocket that sliced through the darkness was a harbinger of chaos, tearing the fragile veil of normalcy that had draped over the city during a period of deceptive calm. The early morning hours brought a haunting silence. Streets that once teemed with the vibrant hustle of life were now empty, save for the occasional wail of an ambulance or the distant hum of a military convoy.

The attack had not only shattered windows, but also the illusion of peace. Schools were closed, businesses shuttered, and the very heartbeat of the city, the everyday comings and goings of its people, was on an indefinite pause. The rockets had not discriminated; they had struck playgrounds and synagogues, markets, and mosques. The pieces of glass littering the streets were as indiscriminate as the hatred that had propelled them.

It was a question that reverberated through the minds of millions. Locals, with an understanding of history, knew that this was but another chapter in a long saga of conflict. But knowledge did not ease the pain, nor did it rebuild the crumbled walls. As the sun rose over Israel, casting long shadows over a landscape marred by the scars of the night, the nation stood at the height of uncertainty. The world watched, some with empathy, others with indifference, as diplomats and politicians scrambled to respond to the crisis.

As the world grappled with the immediate impact of the rockets over Israel, the stage was set for a deeper exploration of a conflict that had, for too long, defined a region and its people. It was not just a recount of a single night's terror; it was an invitation to walk the path of comprehension, to navigate the complex of history, and to emerge with a clearer vision of what it means to seek peace, amidst the echoes of war.

The Gaza-Israel Barrier Breach

In the shadow of the rockets' red glare, a new threat emerged, one that would test the resolve of a nation and the mettle of its people. This was not an assault from the skies but a breach on the ground, a violent rupture of the seemingly unclear barrier that stood as a barricade between Gaza and Israel.

The barrier, a mix of concrete walls, fencing, and advanced surveillance technology, had long been a point of contention. To some, it was a necessary defense against infiltration and terror; to others, a symbol of division and despair. The morning after the rockets fell, it became the scene of a calculated incursion.

In the heart of a small community near the border, the sirens that once signaled incoming fire were now silent—the threat was already on their doorstep. Families who had weathered the storm of rockets now faced a new unknown. The militants' infiltration brought with it a sense of chaos, the kind that turns neighbor against neighbor in a frantic struggle for safety.

Amidst this chaos, a story surfaced, one that would bring the conflict into sharp, personal focus. A young soldier, Avi, had been on patrol near the barrier when the breach occurred. With little more than instinct and his training, he confronted the militants. The ensuing struggle left him wounded, the ground around him stained with the evidence of conflict. Avi's story was not unique; it was echoed in the harrowing experiences of others who faced terror that day. But in his story was a thread of the human spirit a refusal to yield to fear, a commitment to protect home and hearth.

The stakes were higher than ever. The breach of the Gaza-Israel barrier was not just an act of aggression; it was a challenge to the very notion of peace and security. It underscored the fragility of the status quo and the urgent need for solutions that addressed not just the symptoms of the conflict, but its root causes.

As the nation grappled with the breach's aftermath, the path ahead seemed fraught with uncertainty. Would there be retaliation, a tightening of restrictions, a further escalation of hostilities? Or could this moment of vulnerability become a catalyst for change?

The breach of the Gaza-Israel barrier is a call to action—a plea for a future where barriers, both physical and metaphorical, are dismantled. It is a reminder that peace is not a passive state, but an active pursuit, one that requires courage, compassion, and the collective will to transcend the legacy of enmity.

In the pages that follow, we will walk in the footsteps of those who have lived the reality of the Israeli-Palestinian War. We will confront the hard truths and seek out the sparks of hope. For it is only by facing the darkness that we can truly appreciate the light.

Civilians Under Fire

The heat was humid, a cloak of dust and despair seemed to suffocate the city as the sun scorched the land. In the streets of Sderot, normally abuzz with life, the silence punctuated only by the occasional distant boom, or the whisper of tires as a solitary vehicle braved the road. This was a city under siege, its inhabitants bound by an unspoken code of survival that had been honed through years of conflict.

Amidst this uneasy calm, a family of five huddled in a reinforced room that had become their world. The Cohen family: David, a teacher; Sara, a nurse; and their three children, were the embodiment of resilience in the face of an unending storm. Their lives were a blend of interrupted dreams and sudden awakenings, each siren a reminder of the razor-thin line between life and death.

The challenge they faced was not one of their making, yet it defined every facet of their existence. The constant threat of rocket fire from Gaza, which had escalated dramatically since the beginning of the Israeli-Palestinian War, brought a new level of uncertainty to their daily lives. No longer could they take for granted the simple act of walking to the market or sending their children to school.

The Cohen family, like many in Sderot, adapted to this new reality with a quiet courage that belied the complexity of their situation. They fortified their home, practiced emergency drills with their children, and stayed ever vigilant to the warning systems that provided precious seconds to seek shelter.

In the midst of this upheaval, David Cohen found a way

to turn his family's plight into a catalyst for unity and strength. Drawing upon his background in education, he began to organize community gatherings in his fortified home, offering a space for conversation, support, and planning. These meetings became a forum for sharing strategies on how to cope with the psychological toll of the conflict, as well as practical tips for safety.

The results of these communal efforts were palpable. The Cohens and their neighbors forged a network of mutual assistance that ensured no one faced the terror alone. They established a system for checking on the elderly and infirm during alerts, shared resources for home fortification, and even created a shared space for children to play in relative safety.

Reflecting on these developments, it was clear that the spirit of people could not be quelled by fear alone. The community's response to adversity was as much a testament to their tenacity as it was to their vulnerability. They had not chosen this war, but they were determined to face it with solidarity.

The story of the Cohens was not isolated. Across the affected regions, similar tales of courage and cohesion emerged, each a mosaic piece in the larger narrative of the Israeli experience during the war. These stories, while often overshadowed by the broader geopolitical discourse, were critical to understanding the human dimension of the conflict. Their story, while unique in its details, was emblematic of a larger collective experience that deserved to be heard and understood.

In drawing connections to the overarching themes of this book, it is imperative to recognize that the human cost of the invasion is not merely a footnote in the annals of history. It is a stark reminder of the urgent need for a sustainable and just resolution to a conflict that has claimed too many lives and fractured too many families.

Military Engagement

As dawn broke, the horizon was painted with an ominous silence, the prelude to a storm of steel and strategy. The Israeli military, known for its meticulous planning and formidable technology, stood on high alert, prepared to counter the invasion with precision and resolve. The objective was clear: Repel the forces that sought to breach their borders and ensure the safety of the nation's citizens. To achieve this, a well-orchestrated dance of destruction would be employed, leveraging both time-tested tactics and innovative strategies.

Necessary for this military engagement were advanced weaponry, cutting-edge intelligence, a well-trained army, and the iron will of a nation under threat. The materials of war were amassed, soldiers briefed, and the populace braced for the impact of a conflict that would be etched in the annals of their shared history.

The broad overview of the Israeli response was threefold: Defend the borders, neutralize the threat, and maintain the morale of both the troops and the civilian population. This triad formed the bedrock of their military doctrine, a guide through the fog of war. Initially, the Air Force took to the skies with eagle-eyed precision, their jets slicing through the heavens in a display of aerial prowess. Their task was to secure air superiority and provide cover for ground operations. Meanwhile, the ground forces fortified their positions, laying a network of traps and strategic points that would serve as the first line of defense.

The navy, not to be outdone, patrolled the waters, a silent sentinel poised to strike at any seaborne incursion. And beneath the surface, submarines lurked, ready to unleash their lethal payloads upon unsuspecting targets.

Practical advice was dispensed to the soldiers: Stay vigilant, conserve your strength, and remember, the enemy is most vulnerable when they believe themselves safe. Warnings too were given: Do not underestimate the adversary, and be wary of the collateral damage that could turn the tide of public opinion against you.

Troubleshooting was a continuous process, with commanders adapting to the ebb and flow of battle. When communication lines were severed, messengers on motorcycles zipped across the terrain. When ammunition ran low, supply chains worked feverishly to restock the front lines. And when morale wavered, the stories of the Cohens and others like them were broadcast to remind the soldiers what they were fighting for.

But what of the enemy's tactics? They too had their designs, their plans meticulously crafted in the shadows. They dug tunnels beneath the earth, a network of subterranean veins that allowed them to move unseen. They employed guerrilla tactics and hit-and-run assaults that sowed confusion and chaos. And they used propaganda, attempting to fracture the will of the Israeli populace.

As the sun set on this day of conflict, one could not help but reflect on the cost of such engagements. The landscape, once verdant and alive, now lay scarred by the machinery of war. And what of the souls caught in this deadly embrace? The soldiers, their youth consumed by the inferno of battle; the civilians, their lives upended by the whims of war; and the leaders, their decisions etched in the lives of those they commanded.

Hamas: Genesis and Ideology

To unravel the enigma of the Israeli-Palestinian conflict, one must grasp the threads of Hamas with both hands, tugging gently at the fibers to reveal the organization's genesis and ideology. Peering into the heart of this militant group is not just an academic exercise; it is a journey into the entanglement of motivations that propel the enduring strife in the region. Understanding Hamas is crucial for comprehending the Israeli-Palestinian conflict.

Hamas, a militant group, has its roots and ideology intertwined in the region's history, beliefs, and identities. Exploring its origins and principles provides insights into the motivations driving the ongoing conflict. This exploration goes beyond academic curiosity; it's a journey into the intricate web of factors fuelling the region's enduring strife.

This is the setting we must navigate, and to do so, we must familiarize ourselves with the lexicon of the land. Words such as 'Intifada,' 'Mujahideen,' 'Zionism,' and 'Caliphate' are the signposts that guide us through this complex narrative, and it is here that we begin our dissection.

Intifada, a term derived from the Arabic for 'shaking off,' encapsulates a series of Palestinian uprisings against Israeli occupation. The word vibrates with the energy of revolt and the quest for autonomy, echoing through the streets, where stones met tanks.

Intifada, with its roots in the first major Palestinian revolt in 1987, reveals the raw, unyielding spirit of people. It paints a picture of youths armed with nothing but stones and conviction, standing against an armed might that appears invisible. The term becomes a symbol of resistance, a byword for the struggle against occupation.

Mujahideen, which translates to 'those engaged in Jihad,' refers to those who fight on behalf of Islam. The term often evokes images of warriors bathed in the desert's harsh light, fighting for a cause they hold sacred. Mujahideen, a word dusted off from the annals of history and brought to the fore in conflicts across the Muslim world, whispers tales of commitment and sacrifice. It raises questions: When does a freedom fighter become a militant, and who decides which is which? This term is complex, a reflection of the multifaceted nature of warfare and belief.

Zionism is the national movement of the Jewish people that espouses the re-establishment of a Jewish homeland in the territory defined as the historic Land of Israel. A word that, for some, is synonymous with hope and refuge, yet for others, it carries the weight of dispossession and conflict. Zionism, a term that has been shaped and reshaped like clay in the hands of history, often conjures up the image of a phoenix rising from the ashes of persecution.

Lastly, Caliphate, a concept of an Islamic state led by a caliph, political, and religious successor to the Islamic prophet Muhammad is laden with the nostalgia of past glories and the aspiration for a unified Islamic leadership. Caliphate, a concept both ancient and revived, stretches across the collective consciousness of the Muslim world like the starlit skies of old. Its mention brings forth visions of unity and peace under a banner of faith. It is also a concept that has been co-opted, and twisted by some into a justification for dominion and conflict.

Does the mention of these terms not evoke a somber reflection on the complexity of human affairs? Each word is a key, unlocking a chest of historical narratives, religious fervor, and political ideologies.

Hamas, this entity, born from the trial of occupation and resistance, is itself a blend woven from these very threads. Its ideology, steeped in the language of the Mujahideen, draws from the well of Islamic tradition and the narrative of struggle inherent in the concept of Intifada. It is a group that has positioned itself as both the shield and the sword of the Palestinian people, vowing to dismantle the shadow of Zionism and perhaps dreaming of a Caliphate reborn amidst the modern nation-states.

To see Hamas only through the lens of conflict is to ignore the shades of society and politics that color its existence. It is to overlook the schools and the social services it provides, the political governance it seeks to establish, and the influence it wields not just through rockets and rifles, but through ballots and bureaucracy.

In the end, one must step back from the canvas of the Israeli-Palestinian conflict to truly see the role of Hamas within it. The group is both a product of its environment and a shaper of it, a paradox of protection and provocation. It stands as a reminder that in the land of ancient stories and unending conflicts, ideology and practicality are often inextricably linked, and understanding is the first step toward unraveling the threads of enmity.

Chapter 4

HUMANITARIAN HORRORS- CASUALTIES OF WAR

Every sixty-eight seconds, a life is uprooted, a dream is shattered, and a child is orphaned in the land where ancient olive trees bear witness to modern tragedies. This is not just a statistic; it is the visceral reality of the Israeli-Palestinian conflict, a war that has not only redrawn borders but also the very fabric of human lives.

Each step in my journey has taught me to look beyond the surface, to seek the human stories etched into the granular details of larger narratives. So, when I tell you that the cost of this enduring conflict is written in the blood and tears of countless civilians, I implore you to pause and consider the weight of these words.

Why should this matter to you, the reader, who may be oceans away from the epicenter of this strife? Because the reverberations of this war are felt across the globe, in the policies of nations, in the surge of refugees, and in the international outcry for peace and justice. The Israeli-Palestinian conflict is not an isolated chapter of history; it is an ongoing saga that shapes our present and our future.

How does a nation reconcile the need for security with the imperative of human rights? What becomes of the children whose playgrounds have been transformed into battlegrounds? These are not rhetorical questions; they are the urgent inquiries that this book will strive to address.

Let us begin with Mariam, a name that once symbolized hope in a small Palestinian village. Now, it represents a number in the grim tally of civilian casualties. Mariam's story is one among thousands, each a testament to the relentless cycle of violence and the daunting quest for a semblance of normalcy amidst chaos.

The truth is stark, and it is uncomfortable. But it is only by confronting this discomfort, by acknowledging the scale of human suffering, that we can begin to forge a path toward reconciliation and peace. This book is a bridge, a bridge between the disheartening reality of conflict and the potential for understanding and resolution.

Why must we engage with the harsh truths of war? Because, in the end, the cost of ignorance is far too great. It is measured in the stunted futures of the young, in the ravaged landscapes of once-thriving communities, and in the erosion of our collective conscience. We must choose to be more than passive onlookers; we must choose to be informed, compassionate, and proactive agents of change.

The path ahead is fraught with difficulty, but it is paved with the possibility of peace. Through the pages of this book, I invite you to walk with me, to witness the casualties of war not as distant statistics, but as human beings with names, with families, with dreams unfulfilled. For it is in the act of witnessing that we are moved to action, and it is in the pursuit of understanding that we find the seeds of hope.

In the solemn stillness that follows each heart-wrenching anecdote, a question hangs in the air: What can we, as a global community, do to halt the relentless march of suffering? This question is the torch that this book carries, casting light on the paths not yet taken, on the solutions not yet embraced.

As we turn each page, let us do so with the resolve to not only mourn the casualties of war but also to celebrate the resilience of the human spirit. For within the stories of pain and loss are also tales of courage, of communities banding together, of individuals transcending the confines of their circumstances to rewrite their destinies.

The Bombing of Gaza's Al-Shifa Hospitals

Al-Shifa Hospital was the largest medical complex and central hospital in the Gaza Strip, located in the neighborhood of northern Rimal in Gaza City.

The hospital was first established by the government of Mandatory Palestine in 1946 and expanded during the Egyptian and later Israeli occupations. During the Gaza War (2008-2009), much of the media coverage came from correspondents reporting from the hospital. During the 2014 Gaza war, Israel claimed that Hamas militants used the Al-Shifa hospital as a base for their operations, which was denied by hospital staff, including Norwegian doctor, Mads Gilbert.

During the Israel-Hamas war, Israel published animations depicting a large underground militant network beneath the hospital, and on November 15, 2023, its forces raided the hospital, where thousands of Palestinians were taking shelter. Israel claimed that the hospital was being used by Hamas as an operations base, which was supported by the United States. The Israeli raid was widely criticized and Israel was accused by several news outlets of waging a propaganda war. The raid led to the deaths of civilians being treated at Al-Shifa, including preterm babies in incubators. Israel stated that it found a tunnel around the hospital and some weapons inside. However, this did not demonstrate the existence of a Hamas command center.

The Palestinian Red Crescent Society said the strike killed 15 people. UN Secretary-General, Antonio Guterres, said he was 'horrified by the reported attack in Gaza on an ambulance convoy outside Al-Shifa hospital' while World Health Organization chief, Tedros Adhanom Ghebreyesus, said he was 'utterly shocked.' On November 7, 2023, Human Rights Watch determined that the strike was 'apparently unlawful and should be investigated as a possible war crime,' noting that ambulances and other medical transportation must be allowed to function and be protected in all circumstances. It added that the use of ambulances for military purposes would also be against the rules of war, but it had found no evidence of this.

A second Israeli raid on the hospital ended on April 1, 2024, after a two-week siege, which was completely destroyed. Around 300 bodies were found around the hospital, according to the Gazan Health Ministry. A displaced Palestinian said that Israeli 'military vehicles are firing at the hospital buildings' windows, and at anyone who is caught moving between the hallways.'

Hundreds of people returned to al-Shifa Hospital and the surrounding area after the withdrawal. They reported finding bodies strewn inside and outside the facility. Israel has accused Hamas of using hospitals for military purposes and has raided several medical facilities. Critics accuse the Israeli army of recklessly endangering civilians and of decimating a health sector already overwhelmed with war wounded.

"The situation is indescribable, the occupation destroyed all sense of life here."

Schools in the Crossfire

At the dawn of a new day, the sun rises over a landscape scarred by conflict, casting its light on the broken façades of schools, and the empty playgrounds that once echoed with the laughter of children. In this land, where the Israeli-Palestinian conflict rages, the seeds of knowledge struggle to take root amidst the rubble. The main problem at the heart of this narrative is the devastating impact of war on education. It is an issue that bites at the conscience of the world, for it steals not just the present from the youth, but also their future.

The interruption of education is a silent crisis that unfolds in the shadow of the more immediate horrors of war. Yet, its effects are profound, setting off a cascade of consequences that can last for generations. Imagine classrooms turned to dust, textbooks riddled with bullet holes, and the aspirations of young minds snuffed out by the relentless drumbeat of conflict.

In the heart of a land torn by enduring conflict, where the sky often roils with the smoke of battle, there lies a clear comparison between the innocence of youth and the ravages of war. Here, nestled among the olive groves and ancient stones, are the schools of the Israeli-Palestinian landscape, bastions of learning, where children once scribbled their dreams in notebooks, now marred by the scars of relentless strife.

The protagonists of this narrative are children and educators, the unwitting soldiers on an educational frontline. Their adversaries are not merely the tangible threats of missiles and mortars, but the intangible specters of fear and disruption that haunt their daily lives. Among them stands a figure of resilience, Principal Fatima Al-Hassan, who leads a school in East Jerusalem with a resolve that contradicts her slender frame.

The challenge is as cruel as it is complex: How does one provide an appearance of normalcy and education amidst the cacophony of conflict? The classrooms that should echo with lessons and laughter are instead punctuated by the thunderous cracks of nearby conflict, and the very structures that should shelter the minds of the future are targeted, leaving rubble and despair in their wake.

The response to this challenge was multifaceted, a testament to the indomitable spirit of the community. Principal Al-Hassan and her staff devised a strategy to maintain continuity in education. They partitioned the school day into shorter segments, allowing for flexible schedules to accommodate sudden evacuations. Underground spaces were repurposed into makeshift classrooms, offering some appearance of protection when the air above was fraught with danger.

The results, though far from ideal, spoke volumes of the courage and insight of the school community. Attendance, while fluctuating with the receding and flow of hostilities, remained surprisingly steady. Exam pass rates, a tangible metric of academic persistence, defied expectations under such dire circumstances. The school became not just a place of learning, but a sanctuary of stability, reinforcing the fabric of the community against the relentless pull of conflict.

Upon reflection, the approach was not without its criticisms. Some argued that the very act of keeping schools open amidst conflict normalized violence and potentially endangered lives. It is in dissecting these criticisms that broader insights emerge. The refusal to shutter the schools was itself an act of resistance, a declaration that the future of these children would not be forfeited to the present turmoil.

While photographs and charts could vividly capture the physical damage to these institutions, no visual aid could quite encapsulate the mix of fear, determination, and hope that flickered in the eyes of the students as they navigated their disrupted education.

This sample of the Israeli-Palestinian conflict reflects a larger narrative, a narrative of resilience in the face of adversity, and the unwavering pursuit of education as an absolute right. It underscores the universal truth that education is the bedrock of societal growth and the key to unlocking the chains of conflict.

The narrative is not one that ends with the final page of this chapter. It is a story that continues to unfold with each day that passes in the Israeli-Palestinian conflict. As I pen these words, I am acutely aware that the struggle for the soul of education within these war-torn borders is a testament to the enduring power of hope and the unyielding spirit of those who teach and learn against all odds.

It is in these classrooms, amidst the uncertainty and the fear, that the seeds of a more peaceful future are sown. For it is through education that we can transcend the barriers of hatred and misunderstanding, cultivating a generation that may one day bridge the opening of division with the overview board of dialogue and respect.

The struggle for education in the Israeli-Palestinian conflict is a stark reminder that the price of war extends far beyond the battlefield. It is a clarion call for us to stand in solidarity with those who fight not with weapons, but with books and ideas, for a future where the right to learn is upheld as a fundamental human right.

The stakes could not be higher. A generation denied education is a future denied progress. Without the guiding light of knowledge, the shadows of poverty and extremism loom large. It is not merely the loss of academic learning that we must fear, but also the erosion of critical thinking, empathy, and the shared values that education nurtures.

Does the disruption of education in a land far away weigh upon the scales of global concern? Indeed, it does, for the world is more interconnected than ever before. The despair of a child without a classroom today can become the despair of a world facing unresolved conflicts tomorrow.

As we turn the page on this bleak chapter, it is crucial to remember that the power of education is not easily extinguished. There are stories of resilience, of makeshift schools rising from the ashes, and of international efforts to keep the doors of learning open against all odds. These narratives are testaments to the human spirit's refusal to surrender to despair. How do we ensure that the right to education is preserved amidst the cacophony of conflict? The answers to these questions are woven into the fabric of the solutions we will explore together.

In a world where division feeds the fires of war, education stands as a beacon of unity. It is the bridge that can span the chasm of hostility and lead to a future where peace is more than a mere possibility. As a teacher in Jerusalem once profoundly stated, "When we teach our children to build, not to destroy, we plant the seeds of peace."

Psychological Warfare

In the heart of a conflict as enduring and complex as the Israeli-Palestinian War, the psyche of those involved becomes both a battlefield and a barometer of the unquantifiable human cost. As we venture deeper into this complication of suffering and resilience, it becomes imperative to grasp the profound psychological toll exacted on individuals, who are perpetually exposed to the cacophony of war.

Understanding the mental health impacts necessitates a vocabulary not only to articulate experiences that often defy words but also to bridge the gap between the observed phenomena and the visceral understanding of their gravity. Such clarity is not an academic luxury; it is the scaffolding upon which empathy and effective responses are built.

The words that demand our attention and understanding in this context are trauma, dissociation, resilience, post-traumatic stress disorder (PTSD), vicarious traumatization, and coping mechanisms. These terms form the crux of our exploration into the psychological landscape shaped by the relentless storm of conflict.

Trauma, a word that echoes through the hollows of ruined homes and shattered lives, refers to the emotional response to a deeply disturbing or distressing event. This barren definition scarcely captures the aftershocks that ripple through the body and soul, leaving scars invisible to the naked eye.

Consider dissociation, a psychological defense mechanism, often triggered by trauma that entails a disconnection from reality. One might picture a child in Gaza, who, amidst the relentless shelling, retreats into a world within, a place untouched by the terror that besieges his external world. This detachment, while protective in the moment, can fracture the continuity of self, making the task of piecing together a coherent identity, an odyssey in its own right.

Resilience, that promoted quality, images of the human spirit's indomitable will. It is the capacity to recover from or adjust easily to adversity or change, an essential flicker of hope in the oppressive darkness of war. Yet, behind the admiration for resilience lies the unspoken question: What choice remains when the alternative is to succumb?

The term post-traumatic stress disorder (PTSD), clinically sterile, fails to encapsulate the relentless replay of horror that haunts the survivor. It is not simply a label but a daily reality for many Israelis and Palestinians, whose memories of violence are etched deeper than any wound inflicted by shrapnel.

Vicarious traumatization speaks to the silent spread of

suffering, a suffering that affects not only those who directly experience the horrors of war but also those who bear witness. It is the therapist in Jerusalem who, after a day of absorbing the pain of her clients, finds herself flinching at the sound of a car backfiring.

Coping mechanisms, varied as the individuals who employ them, are the strategies used to deal with stress and trauma. Some may find solace in the embrace of community and faith, while others may seek the numbing balm of substances or the solace of solitude.

Now, imagine the resilience of a nation in an example of the mother in the West Bank who, despite the shadow of death, plants a garden of vibrant flowers as an act of defiance and hope. Or the Israeli soldier who, grappling with the ghosts of combat, turns to painting as a vessel to navigate the boiling seas of his psyche.

In these stories, we see the complex fabric of psychological warfare, where each thread represents a struggle, a survival tactic, or a cry for understanding. Through the lens of these key terms, we gain insight into the mental fortitude required to endure, the creativity summoned to adapt, and the silent battles fought long after the guns have fallen silent.

The rhythm of this conflict, with its peak of violence and its quiet of uneasy calm, shapes the minds and hearts of those caught in its pulse. Within this rhythm, we find a resilience that is as remarkable as it is heartbreaking, a testament to the power of the human spirit to endure against unfathomable odds.

And so we delve into the lives touched by this psychological warfare, not as spectators, but as empathetic witnesses to the strength and vulnerability of the human condition. We listen to the stories, the silences, and the sighs, seeking not to solve, but to understand; not to judge, but to bear witness.

To step into the world of those captured in the Israeli-Palestinian War is to enter a realm where the rules of normalcy are suspended, where the line between life and death is drawn and redrawn in the sand, and where the human mind becomes both sanctuary and prison. In this space, the words trauma, dissociation, resilience, PTSD, vicarious traumatization, and coping mechanisms become more than terms; they are the keys to unlocking the depths of human endurance and the complexities of a war, that is as much internal as it is external.

In the absence of a concluding thought, let us simply pause here, in the quiet aftermath of our journey through words and their weight, and reflect on the resilience and suffering that coexist within the fragile human spirit.

Human Shields

In the shadow of a conflict as enduring and complex as the Israeli-Palestinian struggle, there lies a tactic as ancient as warfare itself, yet as controversial as any modern military strategy. This is the practice of using civilians as human shields, a maneuver that blurs the lines between victim and weapon, complicating the moral, legal, and ethical landscapes of war.

A critical analysis of this practice reveals a distressing pattern of manipulation where human life becomes a strategic asset, leveraged to deter enemy action or to sway public opinion. The implications of this are far-reaching, challenging the very foundations of international law and the rules of engagement that seek to preserve some appearance of humanity amid warfare's chaos.

Imagine, if you will, a bustling marketplace, a place of commerce and community where the air is rich with the scents of spices and the sounds of haggling vendors. Now, picture this vibrant scene shattered by the sudden scream of an incoming missile, the explosion tearing through the heart of civilian life. The aftermath reveals a cruel ploy: The marketplace had been used as a shield for militant operations. This kind of scenario is not merely hypothetical; it is a reality that has occurred repeatedly in various forms throughout the Israeli-Palestinian conflict.

To humanize this issue, consider the story of Nusrat, a mother of three, who found herself trapped in her own home, coerced into becoming a part of a living barrier by militants. Her house, strategically located near a key militant outpost, was commandeered, her family's presence a calculated deterrent against military strikes. Nusrat's turmoil is shared by many, her fear and powerlessness a sample of a larger atrocity.

The stakes are alarmingly high, as the use of human shields not only endangers the lives of innocent people but also undermines the principles of just warfare. It forces opposing forces into an impossible decision: to withhold action and potentially allow hostile operations to continue steady, or to take action, knowing it could result in civilian casualties, thus playing into the hands of those employing this heinous tactic.

However, this book is not a mere recounting of grim realities. It is a beacon, guiding the reader through the murky ethical waters to explore viable solutions and frameworks that can mitigate such transgressions. The upcoming chapters delve into the international legal statutes that address the use of human shields, dissecting their efficacy and proposing enhancements. They explore the potential of technology to reduce the risk to civilians, and they examine the role of the international community in enforcing accountability for those who breach the rules of war.

This book will also illuminate the stories of resilience and courage, the untold narratives of those like Nusrat who, against all odds, reclaim their agency and speak out against their oppressors. It will chart a course toward a future where the sanctity of life is respected, even amidst the fog of war.

As we venture deeper into this critical analysis, we must ask ourselves: How can we, as a global society, respond to the moral outrage of using human lives as a tactical game piece? Can we devise strategies that protect the innocent without compromising the pursuit of peace and security? And, perhaps most importantly, how can we ensure that the voices of the afflicted are heard and heeded?

The answers to these questions are not simple, but they are necessary. They demand a confrontation with uncomfortable truths and a commitment to a higher standard of human decency. This book is an invitation to join that quest, to arm oneself with knowledge and empathy, and to take a stand for a world where warfare, though never devoid of tragedy, can be stripped of its most shocking violations against humanity.

In the pages to come, we shall traverse this difficult terrain together, seeking pathways to protect the unprotected and to restore dignity to the most vulnerable. The story of the Israeli-Palestinian conflict is far from over, but through understanding and action, we may yet author a new chapter, one where the term 'human shields' becomes a relic of the past, a reminder of a darker time that humanity has transcended.

Chapter 5

DIPLOMACY AND DEADLOCKS-THE UNITED NATIONS' ROLE

Under the vigilant gaze of a troubled world, the United Nations has stood as a beacon of hope, amid the loud waves of the Israeli-Palestinian conflict. The storied halls of the United Nations have seen an evolving saga of peace efforts, each chapter punctuated by resolutions and debates as numerous as the stars in the desert sky. In the pursuit of peace, the journey has been fraught with Herculean challenges, making the path towards resolution a complex geopolitical intricacies.

In a landscape marked by ancient cities and modern tragedies, the main players of this enduring drama are as prominent as the conflict itself. Israel and Palestine, with their contrasting narratives, have locked horns in a battle for land and legitimacy. Meanwhile, the United Nations, a mosaic of member states, has endeavored to mediate, armed with nothing but the power of collective consensus and the ethos of international law.

The core challenge, as sharp as the dividing lines on a map, has been the enforcement of UN resolutions intended to guide the adversaries toward a peaceful coexistence. The rift between the passing of resolutions and their actual implementation has been wide and deep, shadowed by the specter of veto powers and the often-divergent interests of member nations.

Amidst a cacophony of global crises, the enduring Israeli-Palestinian conflict persists, casting a long shadow on the Middle East. At the heart of international efforts to douse the flames of this decades-long strife stands the United Nations, an entity both lauded and critiqued for its role in mediating peace and conflict around the world.

The claim that weaves through the discourse on the Israeli-Palestinian war is the United Nations' effectiveness or lack thereof in bringing about a resolution. Critics and proponents alike grapple with the palpable tension between the UN's ideals and the on-the-ground realities. The organization's actions, resolutions, and diplomatic efforts have been scrutinized under the microscope of international law, human rights, and geopolitical interests.

Central to the argument for the UN's constructive role is its early involvement in the conflict. Following the end of the British Mandate for Palestine, the UN proposed a partition plan in 1947, aimed at establishing separate Jewish and Arab states in the territory. Although this proposal was accepted by Jewish leaders, it was rejected by Arab leadership, and the ensuing war left the region scarred and divided. Despite the initial setback, this intervention set a precedent for the UN's ongoing engagement in seeking peace.

Delving deeper into this evidence, one finds a UN consistently active in the conflict's timeline. Its peacekeeping missions, such as the United Nations

Truce Supervision Organization (UNTSO), established in 1948, have provided vital monitoring and reports on ceasefire agreements and other security concerns. The deployment of peacekeepers has often been a stabilizing factor in volatile situations, though their mandate and effectiveness have varied with the political climate and cooperation of the parties involved.

However, counter-evidence is plentiful. The UN's resolutions, particularly those from the Security Council, often face criticism for lacking enforcement mechanisms or being subject to veto by permanent members, reflecting the geopolitical tug-of-war beyond the conflict's local parameters. Skeptics argue that these structural limitations hinder the UN's ability to act decisively, leading to a perceived bias or impotence in the face of aggression or violations of international law.

In rebuttal, it's important to acknowledge that the UN operates within the constraints of its member states' interests and that its strength lies in its ability to foster dialogue and provide humanitarian aid. The United Nations Relief and Works Agency for Palestine Refugees in the Near East (UNRWA), for example, has been pivotal in providing education, health care, and social services to millions of Palestinian refugees, thus contributing to the welfare and stability of the region.

More evidence comes from the UN's role in facilitating negotiations. The Oslo Accords of the 1990s, while not a UN-led initiative, received significant support from the organization, underscoring its endorsement of bilateral negotiations and its readiness to assist in implementing agreements.

As the narrative unfolds, one cannot turn a blind eye to the UN's own evolution in its approach to the conflict. From the unequivocal endorsement of a two-state solution to the more recent resolutions condemning settlements in the occupied territories, the organization has shown a capacity for reflecting international consensus, even as it draws ire from various quarters.

In conclusion, the United Nations' stance on the Israeli-Palestinian war is intertwined with the complex fabric of international relations and the conflict's own intricate history. While the UN has been a stage for both triumphs and frustrations, its continued engagement is a testament to the international community's search for peace. Through its multifaceted efforts from peacekeeping and humanitarian aid to political advocacy, and support for self-determination the UN's role, though not without its shortcomings, remains an integral part of the ongoing quest to resolve one of the most awkward conflicts of our time. The assertion of its effectiveness, therefore, is as nuanced as the conflict itself, revealing an organization that, despite its limitations, strives to embody the principles of peace and reconciliation entrusted to it by the global community.

The USA: Ally and Arbiter

Amid the intricacy of international diplomacy, the role of the United States in the Israeli-Palestinian conflict has been as pivotal as it has been controversial. The Superpower's engagement spans decades, a blend of diplomatic overtures, military aid, and attempts to balance its strategic interests with a public commitment to peace. In this chapter, we will dissect a critical incident that epitomizes the United States' intricate involvement in the conflict, drawing insights from the strategies employed and their broader implications.

Set against the backdrop of escalating tensions and intermittent violence, the Second procession of the early 2000s challenged global actors and regional powers alike. It was a time when the Israeli-Palestinian landscape was ruined by a cycle of aggression and reprisals, and the need for a stabilizing force was dire.

The central figures in this narrative were the U.S. government, led at the time by President George W. Bush, and his administration, which included influential voices like Secretary of State, Colin Powell. On the ground, the Israeli government and the Palestinian Authority were locked in a bitter stand-off, with the lives of millions hanging in the balance.

The core challenge was two-fold: to quell the violence that threatened to spiral out of control and to resurrect the peace process, which lay in tatters following the collapse of the Camp David talks in 2000.

The approach adopted by the U.S. was multifaceted. It included high-stakes diplomacy, the leveraging of military aid to Israel as both a carrot and a stick, and the initiation of the 'Roadmap for Peace' a plan aiming to culminate in two states living side by side in peace and security.

The results of these efforts were mixed. The Bush administration's clear endorsement of a two-state solution and the subsequent Annapolis Conference in 2007, which brought together multiple Middle Eastern and international stakeholders, were seen as significant strides toward peace. However, the continued expansion of Israeli settlements and the political split between the

West Bank and Gaza following Hamas's electoral victory complicated the situation.

Upon reflection, criticism of the U.S. role during this period focused on whether its actions were too skewed towards Israeli interests and whether it adequately leveraged its unique position to bring about meaningful concessions from both sides. Connecting this episode to the larger narrative, it's evident that the United States' dual role as Israel's staunchest ally and as an arbiter in the peace process is fraught with inherent tensions. The nation's ability to mediate effectively is often questioned, given its close ties with one of the primary parties in the conflict.

As we ponder the lessons from history, a lingering question remains: Can the United States truly broker peace, or does its bias preclude it from being an impartial mediator? This question segues into the broader discourse on the efficacy of external intervention in regional conflicts. The United States' involvement in the Israeli-Palestinian war is emblematic of the delicate balance between national interests and global peace-making.

We will continue to explore the evolving dynamics of this historic confrontation, probing the roles played by various actors on this loud stage. The quest for lasting peace in the Middle East continues, and as it does, so too does the scrutiny of the United States' role in shaping the future of this storied land.

The European Union's Influence

Amid the turmoil and tragedy of the Israeli-Palestinian conflict, the European Union (EU) has emerged as a significant player, striving to leverage its influence towards a resolution. Through a collage of diplomatic actions and humanitarian efforts, the EU has aimed to thread the needle of peace in a region riddled with complexities. We delve deep into the nuanced role of the EU, unraveling its multifaceted approach to one of the modern world's most enduring disputes.

At the heart of the current issue lies the EU's dual commitment: to advocate for a peaceful resolution while addressing the humanitarian crisis that has stemmed from the conflict. The European Union, unlike individual nation-states, operates as a collective of diverse members, each with its historical ties and political leanings. This collectivity, however, is both a source of strength and a point of contention.

The primary challenge for the EU is to maintain a balanced stance while exerting enough pressure on both Israel and Palestine to move towards a solution. The diplomatic dance is intricate, as the EU must navigate its relationships within the region and with other global powers, particularly the United States.

If this challenge remains unmet, the consequences could be dire. A failure to influence positive change could result in the further entrenchment of divisions, increased violence, and a deepening humanitarian crisis. Moreover, the EU's own credibility as a global peacemaker is at stake, potentially diminishing its influence in other geopolitical arenas.

In response to these high stakes, the EU has proposed a multi-tiered approach. First and foremost is the reinvigoration of an international quad comprising the EU, United States, United Nations, and Russia to mediate the conflict. The EU's diplomatic clout, combined with a more neutral stance compared to the U.S., positions it as a potentially effective intermediary.

The implementation of this strategy involves several concrete steps. The EU has pushed for the resumption of direct talks between Israelis and Palestinians, offering incentives such as economic aid and increased access to EU markets. Additionally, the EU has been a staunch advocate for Palestinian state-building efforts, providing financial and technical support to boost governance and civil society.

The efficacy of the EU's solutions can be observed in past outcomes. The EU's influence was instrumental in the development of the Palestinian Authority's administrative capabilities, and in maintaining a level of economic stability through its generous humanitarian aid.

Some argue that the EU should take a firmer stance on issues such as the expansion of Israeli settlements, using its considerable economic power to impose sanctions or trade restrictions. Others suggest a greater investment in grassroots initiatives that foster Israeli-Palestinian cooperation and understanding.

Why has this land, so steeped in history and heartache, become a crucible for international diplomacy? What lessons can we draw from the EU's dance of diplomacy in this land of contrasts? Employing strong verbs and nouns, let's scrutinize the EU's efforts to heal the rifts. In the bustling markets and along the weathered barriers, the hand of the European Union is subtly present, offering aid, whispering counsel, and beckoning towards a horizon of peace.

Consider the rhythm of negotiations, mirroring the ebb and flow of the Mediterranean waves, that caress the shores of the conflicted land. The EU's strategy unfolds like an intricate melody, with each diplomatic note seeking harmony, but sometimes hitting discordant tones. Incorporating dialogue, let us listen to the words of an EU diplomat: "We stand for peace, for a solution that respects the dignity of all individuals involved. We call upon both parties to return to the negotiating table with open hearts and minds."

In conclusion, the European Union's influence in the Israeli-Palestinian war is a testament to the belief in the power of collective action and diplomacy. The narrative arc of this chapter is one of cautious optimism, a tale of relentless effort amidst a landscape of uncertainty. As we close the pages, we are left with a poignant question: Will the EU's intricate web of influence ultimately contribute to peace, or is it destined to become a mere footnote in the records of a protracted conflict?

Arab World Dynamics

In the volatile theatre of the Middle East, Arab nations have cast diverse roles in the Israeli-Palestinian conflict, each with its underlying motives and strategies. These states, though bound by linguistic and cultural ties, often diverge in their political trajectories and alliances. Here, we embark on an analytical journey, to decipher the complex responses of key Arab nations to the conflict, and to understand how these reactions have shaped the intricate mosaic of regional politics.

The purpose of this comparison is to uncover the layers of complexity within the Arab world's engagement with the Israeli-Palestinian war, dissecting the often conflicting interests that drive each nation's stance.

By examining these variances, we aim to gain a more nuanced perspective of Arab-Israeli relations and the broader implications for peace and stability in the region.

Our analytical framework is built upon several criteria: historical alliances, geopolitical interests, religious and ideological underpinnings, and the interplay of domestic pressures with foreign policy objectives. These benchmarks serve as our compass to navigate through the political landscapes of the Arab countries in question.

Consider, for example, the similar yet divergent paths of Egypt and Jordan, both of which have signed peace treaties with Israel. Their shared border with Israel and their roles as mediators have positioned them uniquely within the conflict. They share the similarity of using their diplomatic channels with Israel to mitigate regional tensions and maintain stability. Their domestic landscapes vary greatly Egypt's struggle with Islamist factions contrasts with Jordan's challenge of integrating a significant Palestinian population into its social fabric. This direct comparison reveals a commonality in strategic aims, but a contrast in domestic sensibilities and political maneuvering.

In stark contrast, the Gulf states, led by Saudi Arabia, have historically maintained a more nuanced and distant stance. However, the undercurrents of change, exemplified by the recent Abraham Accords, have seen certain Gulf nations recalibrate their foreign policies. This surprising shift, a stark deviation from the Arab League's longstanding position, underscores a new Arab pragmatism, sculpted by the desire for technological and economic partnership with Israel, and shared concerns over regional threats such as Iran.

Delving deeper, our analysis reveals broader implications. The Arab responses are not monolithic; they are instead reflective of a shifting paradigm in Middle Eastern geopolitics. The traditional Arab solidarity over Palestine is fraying at the edges as individual states prioritize national interests over collective Arab positioning. This evolution is reshaping the power dynamics within the region and has significant ramifications for the future of Arab-Israeli relations.

What are the real-world implications of these Arab world dynamics? The shifting sands of Arab politics directly impact the lives of Palestinians and Israelis. For instance, the warming of ties between Israel and certain Gulf states may reduce the sense of urgency to address Palestinian aspirations for statehood. On the other hand, it might also bring new players to the table, potentially invigorating stalled peace processes with fresh perspectives and incentives.

Let us paint a vivid image: The bustling cityscapes of Dubai and Tel Aviv, once distant echoes, now whisper possibilities of shared prosperity. Can we envisage a future where these burgeoning ties bring forth a new chapter in the annals of peace, or will they merely overlay the enduring scars of contention?

Why, one might ask, does the Arab world's intricate dance with the Israeli-Palestinian conflict matter? Because, each step taken by these nations reverberates across the deserts and cities, echoing through the halls of power and the homes of the ordinary. The answers lie not in the grand declarations of summits but in the silent shifts of policy and perception that shape the lived reality of millions.

The narrative that unfolds is layered and complex. It tells of ancient lands where the call of the mudslide intertwines with the chime of church bells and the prayers at the Western Wall. It speaks of modern statecraft, where the eagerness for development and security dictates alliances that were once unfathomable.

The story of Arab world dynamics in the Israeli-Palestinian war is a tale of change and continuity, a narrative that continues to unfold with each diplomatic maneuver and regional shift. As we trace the contours of this landscape, we grasp the profound truth: The search for peace is as much about understanding the divergent paths of allies as it is about reconciling the disputes of adversaries. The echoes of this truth resound in every corner of the Arab world, challenging us to look beyond the surface and into the heart of the ever-evolving Middle Eastern saga.

Russia and China

In the intricate chessboard of Middle Eastern politics, where the Israeli-Palestinian conflict continues to cast a long shadow, the roles of Russia and China as external powers are often as consequential as they are nuanced. The involvement of these nations is not just peripheral but pivotal, shaping the strategic balance and influencing the course of events far beyond their immediate borders.

The term 'geostrategic influence' frequently surfaces in discussions about international relations, particularly when unraveling the complex ties between major world powers and regional conflicts. Geostrategic influence refers to the capacity of a nation to use its geographical position, economic leverage, and diplomatic clout to affect the strategies and policies in a specific region or conflict.

This influence is wielded through a variety of means, including trade agreements, military alliances, and diplomatic pressure. It is shaped by the nation's own interests, goals, and the geopolitical landscape in which it operates. The concept has roots in the term 'geopolitics,' a 19th-century coinage that emphasizes the influence of geographic factors in political power. The 'geostrategic' dimension adds a layer of military and strategic planning to this foundation.

In the case of the Israeli-Palestinian conflict, Russia and China's geostrategic influence is part of a broader global power dynamic, where actions in the Middle East can reverberate across international relations and affect their standing on the world stage.

Russia's military presence in Syria and its diplomatic engagements with Iran exemplify its approach to consolidating geostrategic influence. Similarly, China's Belt and Road Initiative, which extends into the Middle East, showcases its strategy of economic expansion and influence-building. One common misconception is that geostrategic influence is solely about military might. While military strength is a crucial component, economic, political, and cultural ties are equally significant in shaping a nation's influence.

Venturing deeper into the Russian and Chinese roles in the Israeli-Palestinian war, one uncovers layers of strategic depth that underscore their respective geopolitical interests. Russia, with its historical ties to the region dating back to the Soviet era, sees the Middle East as a platform to project its power and to counterbalance the influence of Western nations. Its approach is characterized by a blend of diplomatic engagement and military assertiveness.

Can we surmise the subtleties of Russia's involvement without recalling its vested interests in the region's energy resources and its desire to maintain a foothold in the Eastern Mediterranean? The answer is a resounding no. Moscow's support for certain factions within the conflict, its arms deals, and its positioning as a mediator are all informed by these overarching objectives.

In a similar vein, China's emergence as a global superpower has seen it extend its filament of influence into the Middle Eastern theatre. Unlike Russia, China's strategy is less about military presence and more about weaving a web of economic partnerships. Its interests are steeped in securing energy supplies to fuel its burgeoning economy and in creating new markets for its goods and services.

How does China's Belt and Road Initiative fit into this picture? It serves as a testament to Beijing's long-term strategy of economic entanglement, which could eventually translate into a significant political sway. The initiative, which promises infrastructure development and investment, positions China as a benevolent partner to nations, within the conflict's purview. Beneath the veneer of economic cooperation lies a calculated move to cement Chinese influence in a region that is a nexus of global trade routes.

The engagement of Russia and China in the Israeli-Palestinian conflict is not without repercussions. It has the potential to alter the balance of power, introduce new dynamics, and complicate the prospects for peace.

Their involvement is a double-edged sword; it can be a force for stability or a catalyst for further tension, depending on the interplay of their interests with those of the regional actors.

Why would Russia and China invest their resources and diplomatic capital in such a fraught and seemingly out-of-control conflict? The answer lies in a recognition of the conflict's ability to affect global security and economic stability. The region is a crucible, where the interests of numerous actors intersect, and the outcomes have a ripple effect that touches the shores of distant nations.

Imagine the bustling markets of Beijing and the grandeur of Moscow's Red Square. These distant locales are linked by a thread of influence that stretches to the deserts of the Middle East. Their decisions, made in the comfort of gold-plated halls, shape the lives of those dwelling in the conflict's shadow.

The narrative thus weaves a tale not solely of local strife but of global ambition and strategy. As we ponder the implications, we must ask: Will Russia and China be the architects of a new regional order, or will their involvement serve only to deepen the divisions that fuel the Israeli-Palestinian war?

The story of these 'other powers' in the Israeli-Palestinian conflict is complex, interwoven with strands of ambition, caution, and the unyielding quest for influence. As the narrative unfolds, it is clear that understanding their roles is key to grasping the possible paths toward resolution or further entrenchment of this enduring conflict.

Chapter 6

MILITARY STRATEGIES AND TACTICS- THE IRON DOME DEFENSE

*I*n the hushed, pre-dawn hours, the sky over a northern Israeli town was suddenly ablaze with the ominous glow of incoming rockets. Sirens wailed, piercing the silence and sending the inhabitants scrambling for shelter. It was a scene that had become all too familiar, a stark reminder of the persistent threat that loomed just beyond the horizon.

At the heart of this turmoil stood Israel's Iron Dome, an emblem of defense and technological prowess. This missile defense system, a marvel of modern engineering, was about to be tested once again. The stakes were high; failure was not an option.

The main players in this narrative were as contrasting as they were central: the Iron Dome, a sophisticated array of radar and interceptor missiles, and the militant groups, whose arsenal of rockets aimed to sow terror and destruction. The Iron Dome was the brainchild of Israeli defense experts, who, in collaboration with American partners, sought to create a shield that could neutralize the threat of short-range rockets, a daunting challenge that had plagued the nation for years.

The problem was clear-cut: How to intercept rockets traveling at high speeds, often launched in salvos, giving only seconds of warning before impact. The traditional methods of defense were not sufficient against such a threat, which targeted civilian populations and vital infrastructure. A new approach was necessary, one that could provide a near-instantaneous response to an incoming threat.

The solution lay in the Iron Dome's multi-tiered system, a blend of cutting-edge radar technology and interceptor missiles designed to track, target, and neutralize enemy rockets in mid-flight. The system's radar could identify a threat within seconds of launch, calculate its trajectory, and determine if it posed a danger to populated areas or critical sites.

If interception was deemed necessary, the Iron Dome would launch a Tamir interceptor missile, equipped with advanced sensors and steering fins for pinpoint accuracy. The Tamir would detonate the incoming rocket in the sky, far from its intended target, thereby mitigating the risk of collateral damage on the ground.

The results were nothing short of extraordinary. The Iron Dome boasted an interception success rate that was unparalleled, claiming to destroy over 90% of the rockets it engaged. Each interception was a testament to the system's effectiveness, a beacon of hope amid the chaos of war. Civilians could take a breath of relief, knowing that this shield stood between them and the harbingers of destruction.

Upon analyzing and reflecting on the Iron Dome's performance, one could not help but marvel at the ingenuity and resourcefulness that had given birth to such a system. However, it was not without its critics. Some questioned the cost-efficiency of the system, while others argued that it merely addressed the symptoms of a much larger and more complex geopolitical issue. Still, the Iron Dome served as more than a military asset; it was a psychological bulwark, a symbol of resilience in the face of relentless aggression. Its presence reassured the public and demonstrated the lengths to which Israel would go to protect its citizens.

As I ponder the broader implications of the Iron Dome, I cannot help but see it as a sample of the Israeli-Palestinian conflict at large a clash of innovation and determination against the backdrop of an enduring struggle for peace and security. The Iron Dome is not just a defense mechanism; it is a tangible manifestation of the longing for a semblance of normalcy amidst the turbulence of war. It begs the question: Can technological advancements alone pave the way toward lasting peace, or do they simply serve as a stopgap, staving off the inevitable without addressing the root causes of conflict?

The morning's calm was restored, the immediate danger abated, yet the underlying tensions persisted. As we close this chapter on 'The Iron Dome Defense,' let us contemplate the intricate dance of war and peace, technology and diplomacy, and the unending search for a solution that remains as elusive as ever. Could there be a horizon beyond the Iron Dome's reach, where the cycle of conflict gives way to enduring tranquillity? This question lingers in the air, much like the intercepted remnants of a rocket, a silent call to look beyond the immediate and envision a future defined not by the specter of war, but by the promise of reconciliation.

Tunnel Warfare

Beneath the dried-up landscape that sprawls between Gaza and Israel, a hidden complex weaves its way through the earth. Here, in the shadowy confines of tunnels, carved with determination and desperation, Palestinian militants have found a means to circumvent the barriers that stand above ground. These passageways, shrouded in darkness, serve as both a lifeline and a conduit for conflict, fuelling a subterranean war that mirrors the conflict on the surface.

Imagine, for a moment, the sounds of shovels and pickaxes against soil; envision the silent determination of those who delve into the depths, far from the watchful eyes of drones and satellites. But what drives such endeavors, and what peril do they invite?

The tunnel networks have become a symbol of resistance, a method by which militants smuggle weapons, goods, and fighters across tightly controlled borders. These same tunnels pose a significant threat, not only as a means of infiltration for attacks but also as a challenge to any show of lasting peace. They are a physical manifestation of an underground battlefield, where the lines between defense and offense blur in the darkness.

If left unchecked, the ramifications could be dire. Civilian lives on both sides hang in the balance, with the potential for devastating attacks and retaliations escalating an already volatile situation. The tunnels could undermine any progress toward peace, rendering borders leaky and security measures ineffective.

So, what can be done to address this clandestine challenge? Israel has turned to technology and engineering once again, creating the world's first counter-tunnel barrier system. This innovative solution, known as the underground wall, is a formidable structure that plunges deep into the ground, equipped with sensors to detect the faintest whispers of digging.

To implement this solution, Israel has embarked on an extensive construction project along the Gaza border. Crews work tirelessly, embedding the wall with cutting-edge technology designed to provide early warning of tunnel construction. It is a mammoth task, combining physical barriers with electronic surveillance, to create a comprehensive shield against the underground threat.

The preliminary results suggest a significant decline in successful tunnel penetrations. The subterranean wall has not only hindered the construction of new tunnels but has also led to the discovery and destruction of existing ones. This achievement, though considerable, is not a cause for complacency. The architects of these tunnels are persistent and ever-adapting, necessitating constant vigilance, and innovation.

Could there be alternative solutions? Some advocate for a more holistic approach, addressing the socio-economic conditions that fuel the tunnel economy. Others propose increased diplomatic efforts to ease border restrictions, thereby reducing the reliance on tunnels for essential goods. These alternative paths are fraught with political complexities and require a level of trust and cooperation that has been elusive.

The rhythm of this underground struggle is punctuated by the retreat and flow of tension and reprieve. Each new tunnel discovered, each interception of smuggled goods, serves as a stark reminder of the depths of ingenuity driven by desperation and defiance. In the broader narrative of 'The Israeli-Palestinian War,' the issue of tunnel warfare is but one chapter in a complex saga. Here, beneath the surface, the conflict finds new dimensions, challenging the conventional notions of warfare and defense.

One might ask: Can the cycle of tunnel digging and barrier building lead to anything other than perpetual stalemate? Or do these efforts merely address the symptoms of a deeper malaise, a festering wound in need of more profound healing?

As the dust settles in the wake of another tunnel's collapse, a momentary silence falls over the borderlands. It is a silence that speaks volumes, echoing the unspoken hopes and fears of those who dwell above and beneath the earth. And in that silence, a question lingers: What path must be taken to forge a peace that is not buried under the weight of conflict, but rather built upon the foundation of mutual understanding and respect?

The quest for answers continues, as do the efforts to secure a future where children can play without fear of the ground beneath them giving way to violence. Where the promise of peace is not a distant dream, but a tangible reality, unchecked by the shadows of tunnels and the specters of war.

In the search for that elusive horizon, the story of 'The Israeli-Palestinian War' marches on, each step a testament to the resilience of the human spirit in the face of adversity. The narrative of 'Tunnel Warfare' is but one piece of the puzzle, a sobering reminder that the terrain of conflict is ever-changing, and the tools of battle are limited only by the bounds of human ingenuity.

Asymmetric Warfare

In the dried-up expanse, where the geopolitical and historical fault lines of the Israeli-Palestinian conflict run deep, a distinct form of combat unfolds, defying the traditional paradigms of warfare. This is the realm of asymmetric warfare, where the scales of the military might tip not by the weight of numbers but by the cunning application of strategy and the exploitation of the adversary's vulnerabilities.

The Israeli Defense Forces (IDF), equipped with state-of-the-art weaponry and backed by a sophisticated military infrastructure, stand on one side. On the other, various Palestinian factions, including Hamas and the Palestinian Islamic Jihad, operate with a resourcefulness born of necessity, utilizing guerrilla tactics and unconventional methods.

What compels us to dissect this asymmetry? Insight into such a lopsided battlefield can illuminate the evolving nature of global conflict, where traditional power structures are challenged by non-state actors who wield influence through ingenuity and unpredictability. To gauge this warfare, criteria are established: firepower, tactical flexibility, international support, and impact on civilian populations. These benchmarks serve as the foundation upon which a balanced analysis is constructed.

When we lay out the chessboard of this conflict, the IDF's superior firepower is evident. Tanks, fighter jets, and advanced missile defense systems, like the Iron Dome, paint a portrait of overwhelming force. In contrast, Palestinian factions wield rockets, often improvised, alongside a cache of light arms and the strategic use of the aforementioned tunnels. Despite the stark disparity in firepower, the similarities in tactical flexibility surface. Both the IDF and Palestinian militants exhibit adaptability to Israel with its high-tech surveillance and precision strikes, and to Palestinians through their use of urban warfare and the element of surprise.

The contrast sharpens when considering international support. Israel benefits from substantial aid and diplomatic backing from Western powers, notably the United States. The Palestinian factions, meanwhile, rely on a more diverse web of support, often from regional allies, that is less formalized but no less significant in sustaining their campaigns.

Civilian impact is, perhaps, the most tragic measure. In this regard, the asymmetry is painfully clear. Israeli citizens live under the constant threat of rocket fire, their lives disrupted by sirens and the rush to bomb shelters. Palestinians, facing the brunt of retaliatory force, contend with casualties, displacement, and the destruction of infrastructure. This aspect of warfare bleeds into the very fabric of society, leaving deep-seated trauma that transcends generations.

But what do these comparisons reveal? They underscore a fundamental truth of asymmetric warfare: that the imbalance of power does not guarantee a swift or decisive victory. Instead, it often results in a protracted and costly struggle, with victory defined not by territory gained, but by the resilience to endure and the capacity to disrupt.

In today's world, the relevance of such an analysis could not be more pronounced. Asymmetric warfare is not confined to the deserts of the Middle East. It is a global phenomenon, shaping conflicts from Africa to Asia and beyond. Does this reality not prompt us to question the very nature of power and its application? How does a state combat an enemy that thrives in the shadows of conventional might? And what are the moral and ethical implications of warfare where the line between combatant and non-combatant is so perilously thin?

Amidst the rumble of armored vehicles and the whistling of rockets, one-line truths emerge with stark clarity: Asymmetric warfare complicates traditional victory. It demands a re-evaluation of strategies and the recognition that, sometimes, the might of an army is not in its ability to destroy, but in its capacity to adapt and to win hearts and minds.

As readers, we grapple with these complexities, seeking simplicity on the other side of understanding. For in the heart of the Israeli-Palestinian conflict, buried beneath the rhetoric and the rubble, lies a narrative of human endurance of people whose lives are a mosaic of fear, hope, and the relentless pursuit of a day when the word 'war' is a relic of their past.

The pursuit of such questions is as vital as the pursuit of security. As we turn the pages of 'The Israeli-Palestinian War,' let us not forget that history is written by more than the victors; it is also penned by the silent, the suffering, and those who dream of a day when their children will know war only as a chapter in a textbook, long closed and gathering dust on the shelf of a world moved beyond conflict.

Drone Technology

In the shifting sands of the Israeli-Palestinian conflict, the sky has become a domain of innovation and terror, a canvas for the invisible brushes of war. The hum of drones, once an obscure sound associated with far-flung battlefields, has become a familiar refrain in the airspace over Gaza and Israel, heralding a new era of conflict, where the battle for supremacy is as much about control of the skies as it is about the land below.

The history of drone use in warfare is a relatively recent chapter in the annals of military technology, yet its impact has been profound and its evolution rapid. From rudimentary beginnings to the sophisticated silent predators of today, the ascent of drone technology has revolutionized modern warfare, surveillance, and the psychological landscape of conflict.

It was in the early 2000s that the world first took serious notice of drones, or Unmanned Aerial Vehicles (UAVs), as they were employed in the theatres of Afghanistan and Iraq by the United States. These distant cousins of model aircraft quickly transitioned from surveillance tools to lethal weapons, capable of delivering precision strikes without risking pilot lives.

In the context of the Israeli-Palestinian conflict, the use of drones first gained prominence when Israel deployed them for reconnaissance purposes. But the turning point came with the adaptation of drones for targeted killings, surveillance, and intelligence gathering. The conflict's timeline is dotted with incidents where drones have played a critical role, some marked by their success in eliminating high-value targets, others by the controversy of civilian casualties and the ensuing international outcry.

Palestinian factions, though initially lagging in technological capabilities, soon began to employ drones as well, albeit in a different capacity. Their drones, often crudely assembled and lacking the sophistication of their Israeli counterparts, have been used for surveillance, smuggling operations, and even as improvised airborne explosive devices.

The Israeli use of drones is a reflection of a society that prizes technological innovation and has the resources to support it. Conversely, the Palestinian utilization of drones embodies the ingenuity that arises from limitation and the necessity for unconventional methods in the face of a technologically superior opponent.

As the conflict persists, both sides continue to innovate. Israel is at the forefront of anti-drone technology, developing systems to intercept and neutralize enemy UAVs. On the Palestinian side, attempts to circumvent these defenses and enhance the capabilities of their drones are ongoing, a high-stakes game of cat and mouse playing out above the heads of those on the ground.

The proliferation of drone technology has not been without its challenges and controversies. Civil liberties groups have raised alarms over privacy rights with drones' ability to survey vast areas and individuals. Ethical debates rage over the impersonal nature of drone strikes and the potential for collateral damage. Each technological advance brings with it a turning point, forcing both sides to adapt or be left vulnerable.

The skies whisper secrets of war, carried on the wings of drones. They speak of a conflict transformed, of eyes in the sky that miss nothing, and of the looming specter of death from above. It is a chilling reminder that the battlegrounds of today are no longer confined to trenches or urban strongholds.

Is it not striking to consider how a machine, devoid of heartbeat or conscience, has become such an integral actor in the theatre of war? Do these drones, hovering like silent sentinels, not evoke an unsettling vision of the future? As the narrative unfolds, one line stands alone, stark in its brevity: Drones have changed the face of conflict.

In this new age, where a drone can either be the harbinger of destruction or a shield against it, we find ourselves at a crossroads. The Israeli-Palestinian war, with its ever-evolving tactics and technology, continues to be a testament to human innovation and, paradoxically, to human frailty. As we delve deeper into the role of drones in this enduring struggle, let us not lose sight of the individuals beneath their flight paths, those for whom the sky has become a ceiling of uncertainty, where safety and threat are indistinguishable.

In our exploration of 'The Israeli-Palestinian War,' drones stand as a stark emblem of modern warfare, a reminder that the tools of conflict are constantly changing, but the human cost remains a constant, sobering truth.

International Arms Trade

Whispers of metal trade on the wind echo just as ominously as the psychological tactics previously discussed, leading us into the clandestine world of arms dealing that fuels the Israeli-Palestinian conflict. The flow of weaponry to each side is a crucial and often overlooked factor in the longevity and intensity of their war, a thread that when pulled, unravels complex international ties and legal ambiguities.

Under the scrutiny of global attention, one might surmise that the procurement of arms by both Israelis and Palestinians would be a transparent affair. Reality often diverges from such naive assumptions, revealing a murky legal and illegal arms trade. The claim at the heart of this investigation is stark: Despite a plethora of international laws and regulations designed to control the flow of arms, both Israel and Palestine have obtained weapons that have perpetuated the conflict, often with the indirect or direct assistance of other nations.

At the forefront of our evidence is Israel's well-documented military prowess. Its arsenal boasts state-of-the-art technology, much of which originates from foreign shores. The United States, for instance, has been a longtime ally and supplier, a relationship cemented by extensive military aid agreements. The F-35 fighter jets soaring through Middle Eastern skies, and Merkava tanks rolling through the Negev desert are but a few examples of the advanced hardware at Israel's disposal.

Reports from various human rights organizations and investigative bodies reveal that the thread of the arms trade extends far beyond formal agreements. Shadowy networks and third-party deals play their part. It's an open secret that international arms fairs, often with government attendees, serve as marketplaces where connections are made, and the seeds of future arms transfers are sown.

The weapons found in Gaza and the West Bank are often rudimentary in comparison, but their sources are equally contentious. Smuggled through tunnels, transferred covertly via intermediaries, or crafted in makeshift workshops, these arms tell a tale of ingenuity born of desperation. Counter-evidence suggests that international laws, such as the Arms Trade Treaty, are effective in curbing the flow of weapons to conflict zones. However, critics argue that the enforcement of such laws is inconsistent and often politically motivated. The selective application of embargoes and sanctions, some say, is a testament to the power politics at play.

The rebuttal to this is multifaceted. While international regulations have their shortcomings, they have undeniably put pressure on states and manufacturers to exercise greater caution and due diligence. This does not fully address the covert nature of some arms transfers, which can operate outside the boundaries of international scrutiny. As we add more layers to our understanding, we see that private contractors and loose networks of arms dealers also contribute to the circulation of weapons. These actors exploit legal loopholes and the often bulky bureaucracy of international law to conduct their business in the shadows.

A dusty backroom in a country far from the conflict, where deals are struck with a handshake and the promise of plausible deniability. The weapons that emerge from such dealings will leave no traceable lineage, their origins obscured by layers of transactions. But let us ask, who truly bears the responsibility for the weapons that find their way into this war? Is it the manufacturer, the dealer, the end-user, or the international community with its patchwork of regulations? As we consider this, the rhythm of our inquiry accelerates with the urgency of the issue. The arms trade is not a mere backdrop to the Israeli-Palestinian conflict; it is the lifeblood of its machinery of war.

In conclusion, the assertion that international arms trade laws are insufficient to prevent the flow of weapons into the Israeli-Palestinian conflict stands reinforced. The evidence, both overt and covert, paints a picture of a trade that operates on a spectrum of legality, influenced by global politics and economic interests. The challenge remains: to tighten the net of regulations and crack down on the shadow trade that slips through its meshes, all while being acutely aware of the delicate balance of power that these weapons embody.

Cyber Warfare

In a world where the battlegrounds are as digital as they are physical, a new front has opened in the Israeli-Palestinian conflict. Here, in the binary trenches of cyberspace, invisible warriors launch attacks that ripple through societies, economies, and the very fabric of modern life. The main problem that this book addresses is the shadowy yet ever-present threat of cyber warfare a realm where hackers can cripple critical infrastructure, plunder sensitive data, and sow the seeds of discord through disinformation campaigns.

The effects of such cyber skirmishes are far-reaching and can be felt with a severity that parallels any conventional assault. Imagine a hospital reeling under the chaos of a ransomware attack, its lifesaving equipment rendered useless, or a city plunged into darkness as power grids falter under the strain of a cyber intrusion. These scenarios are not mere conjectures they are stark realities in a world increasingly dependent on digital networks.

To personalize the issue, consider the story of a small business owner in Jerusalem. Her entire livelihood came under threat when, one unsuspecting morning, she discovered that her business's financial records had been encrypted by malicious software demanding payment. The attack was part of a larger campaign, targeting the economic underpinnings of the region, indiscriminately affecting lives on both sides of the conflict. This single act of cyber aggression encapsulates the human dimension of this invisible war.

The stakes could not be higher. With the digitization of infrastructure, the potential for catastrophe multiplies. A successful cyberattack on nuclear facilities, water treatment plants, or air traffic control systems could result in unthinkable loss of life and environmental devastation. It is a chilling prospect that a few keystrokes, executed by faceless individuals possibly oceans away, could lead to such dire consequences.

This book does not merely chart the dangers but also offers insights into the complex cyber defense being erected in response to these threats. It delves into the strategies employed by both Israeli and Palestinian cyber units and explores international cooperation in cyber intelligence and security. Do we possess the necessary resilience to withstand and counter these digital assaults? The narrative that unfolds within these pages is one of caution and preparedness. The reader is invited to traverse the clandestine corridors of cyber warfare, to understand the sophistication of modern attacks, and to recognize the importance of robust cyber defense.

The binary codes that underpin our digital reality hold immense power. They can disrupt as effectively as any explosive device, yet they operate in silence and shadows. As we peel back the layers of cyber warfare, we reveal not only the tactics and tools of digital combatants but also the human ingenuity and spirit that rise to meet such challenges. In a world where the distinction between combatant and civilian blurs in the cyber realm, questions of ethics, sovereignty, and international law become increasingly complicated. This book does not shy away from these complexities, but instead, confronts them head-on, offering a nuanced perspective on the digital dimensions of the Israeli-Palestinian war.

Fire and Smoke rise following an Israeli airstrike, in Gaza City.

Israeli security forces inspect charred vehicles burned in the bloody Oct 7 cross-border attack by Hamas militants outside the town of Netivot, Southern Israel.

Israeli soldiers stand by a truck packed with bound and blindfolded.

Palestinians inspect the rubble of the Yassin Mosque destroyed after it was hit by an Israeli airstrike at Shati refugee camp in Gaza City.

Palestinians line up for a free meal in Rafah, Gaza Strip.

Palestinians search for casualties at the site of Israeli strikes on houses in the Jabalia refugee camp in the northern Gaza Strip on October 31.

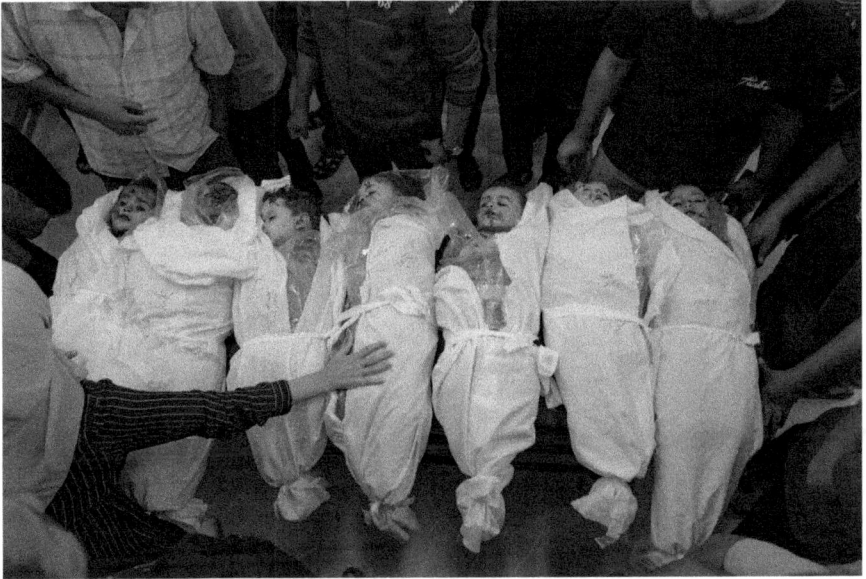

Palestinians stand around the bodies of children killed in Israel.

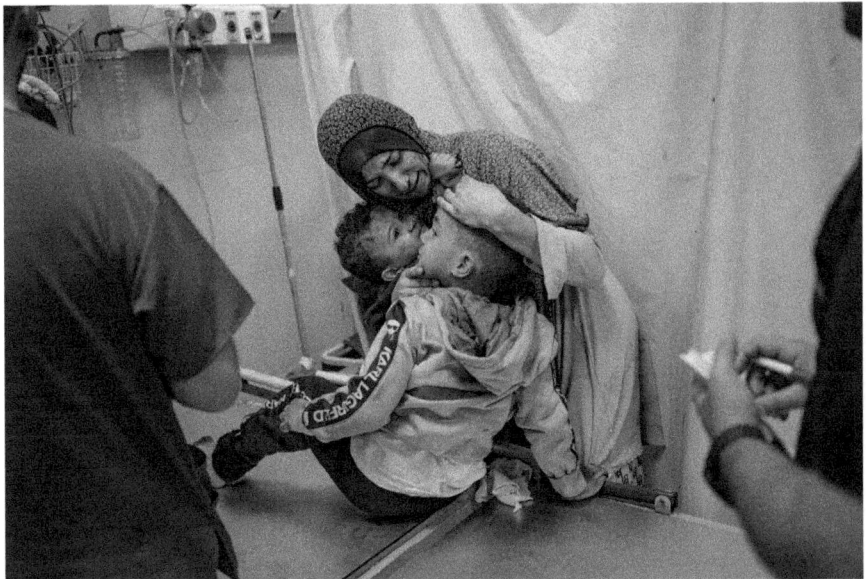

Palestinians wounded in Israeli bombardment of the Gaza Strip wait for treatment at a hospital in Khan Younis.

THE ZIONIST COLONIZATION OF PALESTINE

● Zionist/Israeli locality   ● Pre-existing/Palestinian locality

1882
First Zionist colony Rishon LeZion established under Ottoman rule

1947
Extent of Zionist colonization by end of British Mandate period

1966
Israeli colonization of lands expropriated from Palestinians in the Nakba

TODAY
Israeli colonization of occupied West Bank, Gaza and Golan Heights

VISUALIZING**PALESTINE** | 101   V1 **SEP** 2019 DATA bit.ly/vp101data   Visualizing Palestine WWW.**VISUALIZINGPALESTINE**.ORG/101   VISUAL **1.3**

This aerial view of the makeshift tent camps housing Palestinians.

Palestinians pray over the bodies of people killed in the Israeli bombardment who were brought from the Shifa hospital before burying them in a mass grave in the town of Khan Younis, southern Gaza Strip.

Palestinians gather around the burned and destroyed Al-Shifa.

Palestinian women and child wounded in Israeli bombardment of the Gaza Strip wait for treatment at a hospital.

Chapter 7

THE WEST BANK-OCCUPATION AND OPPOSITION

*I*n the heart of a land steeped in historical reverence and contemporary contention, lies a narrative of modern colonization and its ripple effects. This chapter delves into the intricate blend of Israeli settlement expansion and the profound impact it has on the aspirational peace process, along with the day-to-day lives of Palestinian communities.

The phenomenon in question is no mere footnote in the annals of geopolitical affairs; it is a central axis around which the Israeli-Palestinian conflict rotates. The assertion, then, is clear and contentious: The expansion of Israeli settlements significantly undermines the prospects for peace by altering the demographic and geographic realities on the ground.

Concrete evidence of this claim emerges from the steady increase in housing units, roads, and infrastructure within the West Bank. Data from human rights organizations and international bodies reveal a methodical uptick in settlement activity. This is not just a collection of numbers and statistics; it is a tangible encroachment on land that, for many, holds the promise of a future state.

As we delve deeper, we uncover the stories etched into the landscape, olive groves bisected by security barriers, the steady hum of construction drowning out the pastoral calm. These are not isolated incidents, but part of a systematic effort that has seen over half a million Israeli settlers moving into the West Bank and East Jerusalem since 1967.

Counter-evidence arises from voices within Israel, some of whom argue that these settlements are a legitimate expression of the Jewish people's historical connection to the land, and are necessary for security reasons. They contend that the settlements are not the core issue but rather a symptom of a more profound Arab unwillingness to accept a Jewish state in any form.

In rebuttal, international law and a preponderance of world opinion stand firm on the illegality of these settlements. The Fourth Geneva Convention prohibits the transfer of an occupying power's civilian population into the territory it occupies, a stance echoed by numerous UN resolutions. Moreover, the encroaching settlements often lead to restricted Palestinian access to their own resources, such as water and arable land, and the fragmentation of their territories, which further exacerbates tensions and diminishes the viability of a contiguous Palestinian state.

Additional supporting evidence can be found in the narratives of international diplomacy. Peace talks have repeatedly stumbled on the settlement issue, with Palestinian leaders asserting that continued expansion signals bad faith. The settlements, many argue, predetermine the outcome of negotiations, by creating facts on the ground that are incompatible with a two-state solution.

The answer, while unwritten, is being etched into the terrain with each passing day. The ramifications of settlement expansion are not just lines on a map but lives in the balance.

Palestinian Authority's Role

Amidst the rolling hills and ancient olive trees of the West Bank, the Palestinian Authority (PA) operates with the semblance of a government under occupation. Here, in a landscape where every stone tells a story of past glories and present struggles, the Palestinian Authority attempts to navigate a path laden with both political and societal pitfalls.

The Palestinian Authority, a product of the Oslo Accords, was established as an interim self-government body, aiming to pave the way towards full statehood. Its dominion, however, is a fragmented terrain, where Israeli settlements cast long shadows over its limited sovereignty. This is the stage upon which the Palestinian Authority must perform its role, often caught between the expectations of its people and the realities of geopolitics.

At its helm are figures like Mahmoud Abbas, the President of the Palestinian Authority, and his cabinet, who carry the burden of Palestinian aspirations. Their leadership, fraught with the challenges of governance under occupation, teeters on the line between diplomacy and defiance. The core challenge facing the Palestinian Authority is one of legitimacy and efficacy. It must provide governance and services to Palestinians, whilst under the watchful eye of the Israeli military. This dual accountability has given rise to a complex web of control, where power is both held and withheld.

The strategies employed by the Palestinian Authority have been diverse. From negotiations and international diplomacy to security cooperation with Israel and attempts at economic reform, the Palestinian Authority has sought ways to strengthen its standing and deliver on the promise of a peaceful and prosperous future for its people.

However, the results are often mixed. While there have been successes in education and infrastructure, the Palestinian Authority's reliance on foreign aid and the constraints of the occupation have hampered economic independence and growth. Security cooperation, meant to maintain order, is sometimes viewed by Palestinians as complicity with the occupier, eroding the Palestinian Authority's support base.

In analyzing the Palestinian Authority's role, one must grapple with the comparison of a government-in-waiting against the backdrop of a state that has yet to come into being. The Palestinian Authority's limited success must be weighed against the overwhelming odds it faces, including internal political divisions and a lack of control over borders, resources, and the fundamental levers of power.

The Palestinian Authority's narrative is not an isolated chapter; it is intrinsically linked to the larger story of the Israeli-Palestinian conflict. Its governance cannot be fully understood without considering the broader context of occupation and the quest for Palestinian statehood. The realities on the ground in the West Bank are both a consequence of the Palestinian Authority's actions and the circumstances that constrain them.

The tale of the Palestinian Authority is far from finished. It is a chapter written in real-time, a narrative of resilience in the face of adversity. As the sun sets over the terraced landscapes, casting a warm glow on ancient stone and modern strife, we are left to ponder the future of people and government striving for a place among nations. What role will the Palestinian Authority play in the unfolding story of peace and statehood? The answer is as complex as the histories that converge in this land of prophets and politicians. But one thing is certain: The pursuit of governance amid conflict is a story that demands our attention, for within it lies the seeds of peace or the perpetuation of perpetual discord.

The Palestinian Authority's journey continues, and so does our examination of its role in a war-torn land, where every policy and every decision is a step on the path to an uncertain destiny.

Security Cooperation and Conflict

In the shadow of the age-old conflict, a unique and often misunderstood form of collaboration exists between the Israelis and Palestinians. On the surface, the relationship between the Palestinian Authority and the Israeli government is one marred by deep-seated mistrust and hostility. Yet beneath this veneer of tension lies a network of security cooperation that both sides grudgingly admit is vital for their interests.

The purpose of examining this dichotomy is to unravel the complexities of Palestinian-Israeli interactions and to gain a deeper understanding of the conflict's nature.

It is a relationship that defies simple categorization, one that oscillates between cooperation and confrontation, revealing the multifaceted reality of these two entities.

Setting the parameters for our analysis, we look at the structure, objectives, and outcomes of security cooperation. We explore the shared goals that necessitate collaboration, such as maintaining order and preventing violence, and the divergent objectives that underscore their respective political agendas.

Directly comparing their shared interests, we find that both the Palestinian Authority and Israel have a vested interest in preventing acts of violence that could escalate tensions. The Palestinian Authority seeks to prove its capability to govern effectively, while Israel aims to ensure the safety of its citizens. This mutual benefit creates a space for cooperation, even as broader political negotiations falter.

In contrast, the differences are stark when considering the broader implications of their relationship. For Israel, security cooperation is a means of maintaining the status quo and enhancing its security apparatus. For the Palestinians, it is a double-edged sword; while it offers a degree of autonomy and legitimacy, it also risks being seen as collaboration with the occupying force by the Palestinian populace.

This collaboration provides valuable insights into the nature of the conflict. It emphasizes the pragmatism that can emerge even in the most intractable disputes, suggesting that common ground is not only possible, but it is necessary for survival. It also highlights the limitations of cooperation that lack a foundation in a final-status agreement leading to peace. The relevance of this security cooperation to current realities is undeniable. It serves as a barometer for the level of tension and the potential for violence in the region. Recent escalations or de-escalations can often be traced back to shifts in the intensity and effectiveness of these joint efforts.

One might ask, how can two adversaries work together in such a volatile environment? The answer lies in the nuanced dance of conflicting interests, where each step is carefully measured to avoid tipping the scales toward chaos.

In the bustling streets of Jerusalem and the quiet alleys of Hebron, one witnesses the tangible outcomes of this paradoxical partnership. Palestinian officers and Israeli soldiers, who might face each other in protest by day, coordinate by night to prevent a common foe from disrupting the fragile order. Strong verbs and nouns paint a picture of this uneasy alliance. Cooperation is not about camaraderie but survival; it's not a handshake but a nod a tacit acknowledgment of necessity over preference.

The simplicity in language does not diminish the gravity of the subject but rather makes it accessible to all who seek to understand the intricacies of this enduring conflict. The rhythm of the sentences mirrors the fluctuating dynamics of the cooperation, a mix of short factual statements and longer, reflective observations, that draw the reader into the reality of the situation.

Quotations from officials on both sides add authenticity, revealing the personal stakes involved. "We do not trust them," an Israeli officer might say, "but we need them." A Palestinian counterpart might retort, "Our cooperation is for our people's sake, not for Israel's." Instead of telling the reader about the animosity and shared objectives, this book intends to show them the anecdotes of joint operations that have thwarted attacks or the frustration of Palestinian families who view the Palestinian Authority's actions with suspicion.

The Israeli-Palestinian War is not merely a clash of armies, but interactions that defy conventional wisdom. The story of security cooperation amidst conflict is a powerful narrative that forces us to question our understanding of what it means to be adversaries and allies in a land where the lines between the two are often blurred. It is here, in the day-to-day reality of security cooperation, that we find the most genuine reflections of the conflict and perhaps a glimmer of hope for a future shaped by common interests, rather than divided by enduring hostilities.

Daily Life Under Occupation

In the heart of the West Bank, where olive trees have stood as silent witnesses to centuries of history, there lives a family whose daily existence is a testament to the human spirit's resilience under occupation. The Rahmani family begins their day with the crow of the rooster, a sound that momentarily drowns out the distant hum of military patrols. The children, with eyes reflecting the innocence yet to be marred by the complexities of geopolitical strife, gather their textbooks with care, understanding that education is their silent rebellion against the confines of their reality.

Omaima, the eldest daughter, is a bright spark in the dim dawn; her aspirations to become a doctor are both the melody of her heart and the haunting refrain that keeps her awake at night. Her father, Jawaid, with hands roughened by the labor of the land and softened by the tenderness of his touch, is a mosaic of strength and vulnerability. He knows the barriers standing between his daughter and her dreams are as tangible as the checkpoints they must pass each day.

As the sun climbs, the streets of their village come alive with the rhythm of commerce and the chatter of neighbors exchanging greetings and news, often tinged with the latest tale of a night raid or a detainment. The market is vibrant colors and scents, where the bargaining is as much a dance of culture as it is of necessity. But behind each stall, the sellers harbor the knowledge that their livelihoods are as precarious as the peace they long for.

The unexpected becomes a familiar guest when, one afternoon, a simple walk to the market is shattered by the sound of tires screeching and soldiers shouting. A checkpoint has been erected where none stood before, and the villagers must now navigate this new maze that has sprung from the asphalt. The Rahmani family finds itself at the whim of a soldier's mood, a delay that eats into the day's earnings and the children's playtime.

In the midst of this chaos, a moment of connection occurs a young soldier, his eyes betraying a well of unspoken questions, offers a small gesture of kindness, a shared smile with Omaima. It is a fleeting bridge across the chasm of conflict, a reminder that beneath the uniforms and the roles ordained by circumstance, there is a common humanity.

As the evening prayer call resonates through the village, the Rahmani family gathers on their modest rooftop, looking out over the landscape that is their heritage, their burden, and their home. Here, they speak of the future with cautious optimism, understanding that their daily struggles are but one chapter in a narrative that spans generations. This is the reality of life under occupation, a reality where the resilience of the human spirit is tested by the trials of each new day. It is a life where the ordinary becomes extraordinary, where the act of living is an act of resistance, and where hope is the most precious commodity.

For the reader seeking wisdom, the lives of the Rahmani family and others like them offer profound insights into the endurance of love, the persistence of hope, and the indomitable nature of the human spirit. Theirs is a story not of statistics and political rhetoric, but of lived experiences that illuminate the unvarnished truth of daily existence in the shadow of a conflict that has spanned lifetimes.

As an author, whose own life has been a journey through worlds of conflict and peace, education and enlightenment, the story I share with you is more than an account of adversity. It is an invitation to see, understand, and empathize with those whose lives unfold in a place where the line between survival and surrender is as delicate as the morning's first light filtering through an olive grove.

In the end, the narrative of 'The Israeli-Palestinian War' is not complete without these intimate portraits of life under occupation, where every sunrise is a symbol of defiance and every sunset a promise of continuity. The Rahmani family, and countless others, embody the unspoken truths of a land divided, resilient people, and a hope that refuses to be extinguished.

Non-violent Resistance Movements

In the shadow of the Israeli-Palestinian conflict, a non-violent resistance movement weaves through the narrative of struggle. These movements are the unsung melodies of resilience, harmonizing the desire for peace and justice in a region, often synonymous with violence. The individuals and groups engaged in such acts of peaceful defiance are as diverse as the landscapes that have cradled civilizations, yet they share a common thread: the belief that change can be wrought, not by the might of arms, but by the strength of conviction and the power of words.

As we delve into the heart of these movements, let us first outline the key elements that have come to define non-violent resistance in the Israeli-Palestinian context.

- Boycott, Divestment, and Sanctions (BDS) Movement

- Peaceful Protests and Demonstrations

- Olive Tree Campaigns

- International Solidarity and Activism

- Artistic and Cultural Expression

- Legal Challenges and Advocacy

Each of these points serves as a beacon of hope in a sea of discord, illuminating paths toward a future where dignity and respect are the cornerstones of coexistence.

As a strategy to apply international pressure on Israel to end the occupation, the BDS movement emerged with a simple yet powerful premise: to promote the withdrawal of international support for Israel's occupation policies through boycotts, divestments, and sanctions. This movement draws inspiration from the successful campaigns against South African apartheid, aiming to achieve similar outcomes through similar means.

In the intricate weave of the BDS movement's fabric, one can find threads of triumph. Universities across the globe have divested from companies complicit in the occupation. Artists and musicians have canceled performances, and consumers worldwide make daily choices to support the cause by boycotting products linked to the settlements. Each decision, and each action, contributes to the pressure exerted on the Israeli government to reconsider its stance.

The streets often narrate stories of courage that no book could encapsulate. In villages, weekly demonstrations against the separation barrier become symbolic of the Palestinian spirit. The protestors, armed with nothing but banners and chants, stand in the face of tear gas and rubber bullets. Their steadfastness is a testament to their unwavering demand for freedom and justice.

These peaceful gatherings, while at times met with harsh responses, have attracted international attention, drawing support from activists and human rights organizations. The message is clear: The quest for peace does not rest on the laurels of silence, but it rises on the winds of vocal, yet non-violent, dissent.

The olive tree, an ancient symbol of peace and resilience, has become a canvas for non-violent resistance. Through campaigns like 'Keep Hope Alive' and the 'JAI Olive Tree Campaign,' the Joint Advocacy Initiative of Palestinians and international volunteers join hands to plant olive trees. These trees are more than just plants; they are living symbols of Palestinians' connection to their land and their determination to reclaim their rights and livelihoods. Even as settlers and soldiers uproot these trees, the campaigns persist, a cycle of planting and replanting that mirrors the cycle of struggle and renewal inherent to the Palestinian experience.

From the International Solidarity Movement (ISM) to the Free Gaza Flotilla, international activists have played a pivotal role in non-violent resistance. Their presence brings global attention to the plight of the Palestinians and often helps to moderate the actions of the Israeli military. These activists stand side by side with Palestinian communities, sharing their hardships and amplifying their voices. Their involvement is a bridge between worlds, a tangible connection that empowers local communities and challenges the international community to move beyond mere observation to active participation.

Art is resistance. In the murals that adorn the separation wall, the poems that reverberate in the hearts of the oppressed, and the music that flows through the alleys of refugee camps, there is a powerful assertion of identity and a refusal to be silenced. Palestinian artists like Banksy and poets like Mahmoud Darwish have brought the world's eyes to the canvas of their struggle, painting it with the colors of their culture and the strokes of their longing for freedom. Through these expressions, the narrative of the Palestinian people is shared, a narrative that humanizes and transcends the statistics and headlines.

The battle for rights and recognition is also fought in the courts. Legal advocacy groups, both Palestinian and international, employ the tools of international law to challenge injustices. They represent detainees, contest land confiscations, and bring cases to international bodies, striving for accountability and the rule of law. These legal efforts shine a light on the discrepancies between the policies of occupation and the principles of international law, urging the world to recognize and rectify these disparities.

As we journey from one form of non-violent resistance to another, we see a landscape punctuated not by the smoke of gunfire, but by the quiet fires of determination. These movements, with their diverse tactics and shared ethos, compose a narrative of non-violent resistance that is as compelling as it is essential to understanding the Israeli-Palestinian conflict.

They stand as a reminder that even in the darkest of times, there are those who choose the light of peace over the shadows of war. It is within these stories of non-violent resistance that we find not only the seeds of change but also the fertile soil in which they are sown.

Fatah and Hamas: Unity and Division

In delving into the intricate narrative of 'The Israeli-Palestinian War,' it becomes apparent that comprehending the internal dynamics of Palestinian politics is as crucial as understanding the external struggle for statehood. At the heart of this internal landscape are Fatah and Hamas, two factions whose unity and division have oscillated with the retreat and flow of political tides. Their relationship is not just a side note, but a central thread that weaves through the fabric of the Palestinian quest for sovereignty.

To navigate this narrative, one must first acquaint oneself with a lexicon of terms that are pivotal to the discourse. These terms include Fatah, Hamas, the Palestinian Authority, the Oslo Accords, the Unity Government, and the Quartet Conditions. These words, seemingly arcane to the uninitiated, are keys that unlock a deeper understanding of the Palestinian plight.

Fatah, originating from a reverse acronym of 'Harakat al-Tahrir al-Watani al-Filastini,' meaning 'The Palestinian National Liberation Movement,' was founded in the late 1950s. It emerged primarily as a secular movement with the aim of liberating Palestinian land and has been a dominant force within the Palestine Liberation Organization (PLO).

Conversely, Hamas, an acronym for 'Harakat al-Muqawama al-Islamiyya' (The Islamic Resistance Movement), was born in 1987 amidst the First Procession. Its identity is rooted in Islamic principles, and it gained a reputation for its military resistance against Israeli occupation, as well as for its social welfare programs.

The Palestinian Authority (PA), established as part of the Oslo Accords, serves as a semi-autonomous governing body with limited control over parts of the West Bank and Gaza Strip. It is seen as a provisional entity, with the ultimate goal of becoming the government of a fully sovereign Palestinian state.

The Oslo Accords, a series of agreements signed in the 1990s between Israel and the PLO, were intended to pave the way for peace and the eventual creation of a Palestinian state. These accords were a milestone in

Fatah's strategy of negotiation, contrasting sharply with Hamas's approach to armed resistance.

The Unity Government refers to the coalition government formed between Fatah and Hamas in an attempt to reconcile their differences and present a united front in dealings with Israel and the international community. The union, however, has been fraught with challenges and intermittent breakdowns.

Lastly, the Quad Conditions, set forth by the Quartet on the Middle East (comprising the UN, the US, the EU, and Russia), were designed to guide the peace process. These conditions include the recognition of Israel, adherence to previous agreements, and the renunciation of violence, which particularly affected Hamas's international standing and acceptance.

Imagine the bustling streets of Ramallah, where the yellow flags of Fatah flutter alongside the green banners of Hamas. The imagery is powerful, evoking the fervor of political activism. These symbols, ubiquitous across the Palestinian territories, are as much a declaration of intent as they are an appeal to the hearts and minds of the populace.

How does one reconcile the two? Fatah's secular nationalism and Hamas's Islamic ideology appear as divergent as the day is long. Yet, they share the common soil of Palestinian identity, rooted deeply in the longing for self-determination. Imagine the olive farmer in the West Bank, tending to trees that have stood for generations, or the fisherman in Gaza, casting his net into the Mediterranean's blue expanse. Their aspirations are mirrored in the politics of Fatah and Hamas, each vying to shape the Palestinian future.

In the end, the narrative of Fatah and Hamas is not one to be concluded with definitive statements or rhetorical flourish. It is a story still being written, its chapters filled with the aspirations of people and the harsh realities of a conflict that has spanned generations. The tale of these two factions is woven with threads of hope and despair, a chronicle of the Palestinian spirit that continues to endure against all odds.

Chapter 8

THE ISRAELI POLITICAL ARENA-INTERNAL FRONT

*A*midst the noisy landscape of the Middle East, the fabric of Israeli society has been persistently tested by the winds of war. The most recent chapter in this enduring conflict not only redraws the lines in the sand but also leaves a lasting imprint on the mosaic of Israeli politics. The reverberations of war resonate through the bustling streets of Tel Aviv, whisper across the ancient stones of Jerusalem, and echo in the hushed corridors of power.

As dawn breaks over the Jerusalem skyline, casting a golden hue upon the city, the air is thick with the anticipation of change. The main players in this intricate political drama are as varied as the land itself. The core challenge erupting from the ashes of conflict is the shifting public opinion. A nation once united under the banner of security and survival now finds itself fragmented, with divergent ideas about the path forward. The populace, caught between the desire for peace and the reality of perpetual threat, looks to its leaders for direction.

In response to this existential dilemma, a new approach emerged, one that would require the finesse of diplomacy balanced with the unwavering strength of military resolve. Leaders, both military and civilian, crafted strategies aimed at preserving the nation's integrity, while seeking to placate a war-weary public. They engaged not only in the art of warfare but also in the theatre of public sentiment, orchestrating a symphony of policies designed to maintain a delicate equilibrium.

The results of these endeavors, while not immediately apparent, began to surface in the form of shifting allegiances and emerging political blocs. Data, the lifeblood of any political campaign, showed a populace more inclined to support leaders, who promised stability with a hint of progress toward peace, rather than the traditional hardline stance.

Reflecting on these loud times, one cannot help but recognize the intricate dance between power and principle. Criticisms abound, with detractors quick to point out the perceived shortcomings of any chosen path. In the crucible of conflict, the Israeli political arena has proven itself to be a dynamic beast, capable of both violent upheaval and inspiring unity. The case of Israel's political transformation serves as an example of the larger narrative of perseverance and adaptation. It is a testament to the nation's ability to endure, to bend without breaking under the weight of existential threats.

Home Front Resilience

In the heart of a nation accustomed to the drumbeat of conflict, the Israeli home front stands as a testament to resilience. Here, in the bustling markets and quiet neighborhoods, the spirit of a community galvanized by adversity takes shape. It is a canvas painted with the broad strokes of unity and the fine lines of individual courage, each thread woven into the fabric of Israeli society. The concept of civilian response in Israel is not merely a matter of policy; it is the lifeblood of the nation. Rooted in a history of overcoming siege and strife, Israelis have developed a unique ecosystem of support and emergency preparedness that serves as both shield and sanctuary.

Take, for example, the communal bomb shelters that pepper the landscape. These are not cold, desolate halls of concrete and steel, but rather vibrant hubs of solidarity. In times of crisis, they transform into gathering places where the young and old share stories, where the anxious find comfort, and where the spirit of camaraderie dispels the shadow of fear. These shelters are not just a physical refuge, but a symbol of collective resolve.

The resilience of the Israeli home front is further exemplified by the role of community networks. Local councils and neighborhood committees are not mere administrative units, but the beating heart of preparedness. They orchestrate drills, disseminate critical information, and, most importantly, tailor their strategies to the unique needs of their constituents. These networks are the threads that bind the fabric of society, ensuring that no individual stands alone against the tide of uncertainty.

Consider the city of Sderot, located a mere stone's throw from the Gaza border. Here, residents have, over time, adapted to a routine punctuated by the threat of rocket fire. Playgrounds are equipped with bomb-proof shelters, and schools conduct regular emergency drills. The city's architecture itself speaks to this adaptation, with reinforced safe rooms being as commonplace as balconies in other locales.

Data from the Israeli Home Front Command reveals the depth of this preparedness. Surveys indicate that a remarkable percentage of the population is aware of the nearest shelter and has access to emergency kits stocked with essentials. This level of readiness doesn't emerge overnight; it is the fruit of ongoing education and drills that instill a sense of readiness without succumbing to panic.

The varied demographics of Israeli society mean that perspectives on preparedness and response can differ vastly. The stoic determination of a community in the north may contrast with the anxious diligence of a family in Tel Aviv. Understanding these nuances is crucial, for it is within these differences that the true strength of the Israeli home front is found in a mosaic of approaches and attitudes that together form an unbreakable whole.

Amidst this landscape of preparedness, it is vital to clarify terms that might otherwise seem arcane. 'Collective protection' refers not just to the physical measures like shelters and Iron Dome systems, but also to the psychological armor forged through shared experience. 'Resilience' goes beyond mere survival; it encompasses the ability to bounce back, to support one another, and to continue living with purpose and joy, even under the shadow of conflict.

As we draw the curtains on this exploration, let us distill the essence of what has been laid bare. The Israeli home front is a fortress not of bricks and mortar but of unwavering spirit and mutual support. It is an ever-evolving organism that adapts to the relentless rhythm of the region's heartbeat.

What then are the key takeaways from this glimpse

into the Israeli civilian response to conflict? It is the understanding that preparedness is both a practical endeavor and a cultural ethos. It is the recognition that, in the trial of conflict, a community can forge bonds that are as strong as steel. And it is the realization that, in the dance of war and peace, resilience is the melody that ensures the music plays on, even when the notes are fraught with tension.

The streets may be quiet now, as the echoes of turmoil fade into the night, but the resilience of the Israeli home front remains, a silent guard, watching over the nation as it navigates the complexities of its existence. And so, the question beckons, whispered on the winds of the hustle. How will this resilience shape the future of people who have become masters of standing firm in the face of adversity? Only time will tell, but one thing is certain, the resilience of the Israeli home front will endure a beacon of hope in a tumultuous world.

Military Ethos and National Service

In Israeli society, where the past and present interweave, the Israeli Defense Forces (IDF) emerge as a central thread, binding the nation's people with an ethos of service and defense. The IDF is not merely a military institution; it is an ordeal where citizenship and service fuse, where young men and women are sculpted into guardians of their homeland.

Embarking on this exploration, words like 'induction,' 'military ethos,' and 'national service' are more than terms; they are the embodiment of an ideal, the lifeblood coursing through the veins of the nation. Induction, military ethos, national service, reservist duties, and the people's army are the key phrases that unlock the door to a deeper understanding. These terms are not just words on a page; they are the reflection of a nation's soul, the blueprint of its resilience.

Induction, or mandatory military service, is the call that every Israeli hears, a rite of passage that beckons at the cusp of adulthood. It is the equalizer, bringing together individuals from diverse backgrounds, each contributing to the defense of their shared home. This practice is not unique to Israel, but the Israeli approach to conscription is distinctive; it is woven into the societal fabric, a common experience that shapes identity and citizenship.

The term 'military ethos' captures the spirit that the IDF instills in its service members. It is a set of values that includes discipline, camaraderie, sacrifice, and a profound sense of responsibility towards one's fellow citizens and country. These values bleed into civilian life, influencing the national character and ensuring that the military's impact extends far beyond the battlefield.

National service, while often used interchangeably with conscription, encompasses a broader scope. It is the manifestation of civic duty, where service to the country can take many forms, including but not limited to, military engagement. For some, it may involve contributing to civilian sectors such as education, healthcare, and social welfare, offering an alternative route to fulfilling their national responsibilities.

Reservist duties call upon the experienced to stand ready, to return to service when the nation calls. This continued commitment epitomizes the ongoing bond between the individual and the state, a reminder that service does not end with the completion of conscription.

The concept of a 'people's army' encapsulates the IDF's unique nature. It is an army that draws its strength from the populace, an embodiment of the nation itself. In this model, there is no distinction between the soldier and the civilian; they are one and the same, each individual a guardian of their homeland.

These concepts find echoes in the familiar. Conscription can be linked to the universal experience of schooling, a structured, formative period that prepares the young for the challenges ahead. Military ethos shares the values found in tight-knit communities, where solidarity and mutual aid are not just principles, but practices. National service parallels the contribution every citizen makes to society, be it through work, volunteering, or simply being an active member of the community.

The IDF's role in society is multifaceted, simultaneously an armed force and a national institution that fosters unity, discipline, and a sense of purpose. Its presence in the lives of Israelis can be seen in the way former soldiers draw on their military experiences in their civilian careers, applying the leadership skills and resilience they've honed to a multitude of fields. In a land where history's shadow looms large, the IDF stands as a barricade, a promise to future generations that their heritage will be safeguarded. It is a pledge of security and a commitment to prosperity, ensuring that the nation's heartbeat continues unabated. They are not just components of a military system; they are the reflection of a society's soul, the resolute affirmation of people determined to survive and thrive amidst the complexities of modern nationhood.

In the silence that follows this contemplation, one can almost hear the soft footfalls of soldiers on patrol, the hushed conversations of families discussing their loved one's service, and the unspoken acknowledgment that every citizen is, in their own way, a guardian of the state. This is the essence of the IDF's role in Israeli society, a role that transcends the uniform and becomes a defining feature of national identity.

Economic Strains and Stability

As the dawn breaks over the horizon, the golden hues of the Middle Eastern sun cast a warm glow on the bustling marketplaces and high-tech office parks of Israel. Beneath this veneer of normalcy, the Israeli economy faces the relentless undercurrents of conflict with its Palestinian neighbors. The echoes of this enduring conflict reverberate through the financial districts and olive groves alike, shaping an economic landscape fraught with challenges and uncertainties.

At the heart of this economic saga lies a pressing challenge: The sustained Israeli-Palestinian conflict has imposed a significant burden on Israel's economy. The cost of continuous military operations, defense spending, and the impact on international trade relationships weigh heavily on the nation's financial well-being. The question looms large: What are the potential consequences if these economic strains are left unchecked, and what strategies could be employed to steer the nation toward stability and growth?

The consequences of inaction are manifold and ominous. If the economic ramifications of the conflict are not addressed, Israel may face a future where the high costs of security and defense begin to erode the foundations of its once-thriving economy. The rising defense budget could crowd out vital investments in education, infrastructure, and technology, stunting the potential for innovation and growth. International investors, wary of instability, might divert their capital elsewhere, leading to a decline in foreign direct investment. Moreover, the specter of unemployment could rise, as businesses struggle to cope with the uncertainties of an economy overshadowed by conflict.

To navigate these treacherous waters, a multipronged solution is imperative. One such strategy is the boost of economic ties with neighboring countries and the international community, fostering relationships that transcend the geopolitical rifts. By engaging in regional cooperation and trade agreements, Israel can create economic interdependencies that not only drive growth but also contribute to a climate of stability and peace.

Implementing this strategy begins with the establishment of economic corridors and free trade zones that encourage commerce and investment. Initiatives like the Qualifying Industrial Zone (QIZ) agreement, which allows goods produced in Israel and neighboring countries to enter the United States duty-free, could be expanded and replicated. Collaborative ventures in sectors such as renewable energy, water conservation, and agriculture have the potential to yield mutual benefits, fostering a sense of interdependence and shared prosperity.

Evidence of the efficacy of these approaches can be seen in past successes. The QIZ initiative has already led to an increase in exports and job creation, demonstrating that economic collaboration can pave the way for peace dividends. Moreover, Israel's burgeoning technology sector, often dubbed the 'Startup Nation,' stands as a testament to the transformative power of investment in innovation a sector that could further flourish under the wings of regional cooperation.

While these solutions offer a path forward, alternative strategies merit consideration as well. For instance, increasing public-private partnerships (PPPs) could serve to alleviate the financial burden on the government while mobilizing private sector expertise and resources. Additionally, fostering a culture of entrepreneurship and supporting small and medium-sized enterprises (SMEs) could further insulate the economy from the shockwaves of conflict.

Would it be too optimistic to envision a future where the barriers of conflict are dismantled to make way for bridges of economic cooperation? Perhaps. Yet, history has shown that economies can be powerful engines for peace, and in the case of Israel, economic resilience might just be the key to unlocking a more stable and prosperous future.

The narrative of Israel's economy is thus a complex interplay of resilience and vulnerability, of innovation amidst adversity. As the sun sets, casting long shadows over the land, one ponders the path ahead. Will the olive branches of economic collaboration intertwine with the laurels of peace, or will the weight of war continue to choke the nation's economic breath? The answer lies not in the stars, but in the collective will of people determined to forge stability from the crucible of conflict.

Israel's Technological Edge in Warfare

In the barren expanse of the Negev Desert, where the unforgiving sun scorches a terrain that has witnessed centuries of conflict, a new chapter of warfare is being written. This is a tale not of brute force, but of the cunning application of technology, a strategic saga that unfolds within the complex narrative of the Israeli-Palestinian conflict.

Within this modern theatre of conflict, Israel, a nation born from the ashes of the Holocaust and hardened by the relentless reality of existential threats, has emerged as a technological titan. Its adversaries are often less equipped than conventional forces or asymmetric threats like insurgent groups. Yet the Israeli Defense Forces (IDF) navigate this landscape with a blend of innovation and adaptability that has become the hallmark of their military strategy.

The main players in this case are as diverse as the technology they wield. They range from the engineers who conceive cutting-edge defense systems to the soldiers who deploy them, and the political leaders whose decisions shape their use.

The challenge at the heart of this narrative is the constant pressure of asymmetric warfare, where a conventional army like the IDF faces opponents that do not conform to traditional battle lines. These adversaries often employ guerrilla tactics, launching rockets from civilian areas, and utilizing underground networks to stage attacks. The asymmetric nature of this conflict demands a response that is both precise and preventative, a task that falls squarely on the shoulders of technological innovation.

Israel's approach has been to invest heavily in a multi-tiered defense system. Iron Dome, David's Sling, and the Arrow missile defense systems are the cornerstones of this strategy. These technologies are not mere shields; they symbolize a philosophy of proactive defense that seeks to neutralize threats before they can inflict harm. The results of this approach are tangible. The Iron Dome, with its radar-guided kinetic interceptors, has boasted a success rate exceeding 90 percent, saving countless lives by intercepting incoming projectiles before they can strike Israeli soil. David's Sling and the Arrow systems provide additional layers of protection, targeting longer-range threats and ballistic missiles.

However, to analyze this through an unblemished lens would be to ignore the criticisms and complexities inherent in such strategies. Questions arise about the long-term sustainability of a defense-centric posture and the moral quandaries presented by the intermingling of combatants and non-combatants in densely populated areas. These are considerations that must be weighed with careful reflection.

This focus on defense technology is but one aspect of a larger narrative concerning Israel's overall technological edge in warfare. Unmanned aerial vehicles (UAVs), cyber warfare capabilities, and intelligence-gathering systems exemplify the breadth of Israel's tech-centric approach to modern conflict.

In closing this examination, one cannot help but ponder a broader question: Can technological superiority alone forge a path to lasting peace, or is it merely a stopgap, a means to provide security while the search for a political resolution continues? This thought lingers, inviting readers and policymakers alike to engage with the complex interplay of technology, warfare, and diplomacy.

Cultural Impact of Conflict

In the heart of bustling Tel Aviv, where the city's pulse beats in sync with the rhythm of daily life, there sits a small, unassuming café. Its walls, coated with layers of mismatched paint, tell stories of a country perpetually in flux.

In literature, writers delve into the depths of collective memory, their prose a conduit for the stories that must be told and retold. Through their words, the narratives of the war take on new dimensions, allowing readers to traverse the landscapes of the past and present, to feel the grit of the desert and the sorrow of a mother's tears. These tales are not just for the people of Israel and Palestine; they resonate with anyone who has ever yearned for an appearance of understanding amidst chaos.

The emotional echo of the conflict reverberates through collective memory. Public holidays and memorials are not merely dates on a calendar; they are the stitches in the fabric of society, binding together a nation with the thread of shared history. The unexpected journey of this war has led to a surprising turn in the way Israelis perceive their identity, their art becoming a lens through which the world can glimpse their soul. They are lessons of endurance, the power of cultural expression to heal, and the relentless pursuit of beauty amidst the ugliness of war.

The art, music, and literature that have blossomed from this land of contrasts are not simply the products of individual talent. They are the collective heartbeat of people who have learned to channel their pain into creation, to find unity in their diversity, and to make their voices heard through the universal language of culture. This is the story of the cultural impact of the Israeli-Palestinian War, a tale of how, even in the darkest of times, humanity's enduring light refuses to be extinguished.

Chapter 9

ECONOMIC IMPACTS- THE COST OF CONFLICT

*I*n the heart of the Middle East, where ancient narratives interweave with modern-day geopolitics, the Israeli-Palestinian conflict stands as a testament to a century's struggle, not just over land, but over the very essence of identity and survival. At the core of this enduring conflict lies a cost, often overshadowed by the more immediate human toll. This is the financial burden that weighs heavily on both the Israeli and Palestinian economies.

Have you ever stopped to consider the true economic impact of such a prolonged conflict? The narrative often fixates on the loss of life and the political turmoil, but beneath the surface, there is a relentless financial hemorrhage affecting millions. The assertion at hand is clear: The Israeli-Palestinian conflict has levied a substantial economic cost on both nations, draining resources, hindering growth, and perpetuating a state of fiscal uncertainty.

Consider, for instance, the defense spending of Israel. A considerable portion of the national budget is allocated to military expenditure. In 2020, Israel's defense budget stood at approximately $20.5 billion, a figure that represents about 5.6% of its GDP. The ripple effect of this spending is vast resources that could potentially foster innovation or social welfare programs are instead channeled into maintaining the status quo of security.

Venture deeper into this expenditure and you will find that the costs are not merely numbers on a balance sheet. They are missed opportunities for societal advancement, education reform, and healthcare improvements. The high taxes required to support defense spending leave businesses and individuals with less disposable income, which in turn affects domestic consumption and overall economic vitality.

However, there lies a counter-narrative. Some argue that military spending acts as an economic stimulus, creating jobs and fuelling technological advancements with civilian applications. Israel's robust defense industry is a case in point, contributing to the nation's exports and innovation landscape. Turning to the Palestinian economy, the constraints are even more pronounced. Restrictions on movement, access to resources, and the blockade of Gaza have choked economic activities. The World Bank estimated that the Palestinian economy could add $3.4 billion to its GDP annually if it had full access to Area C of the West Bank, an area currently under Israeli control.

The counter-evidence here may highlight the complexities of security concerns and the rationale behind certain restrictions. Yet, this clarification is necessary: The economic impact on the Palestinian side is not a mere by-product of security measures, but a consequence of prolonged uncertainty and lack of sovereignty.

What happens when an economy is shackled by such constraints? Unemployment soars, and with it, the specter of poverty. Infrastructure crumbles and foreign investment becomes a mirage on the horizon of a desert of economic desolation.

To further substantiate the financial toll, consider the international aid sent to support the Palestinian territories. This aid, while vital, is often a calming rather than a cure, fostering dependency instead of self-reliance. The potential for a thriving Palestinian economy exists, but it remains a seed in unyielding soil, watered with uncertainty and choked by conflict.

In conclusion, the narrative of the Israeli-Palestinian conflict is incomplete without acknowledging the clear economic realities it has cultivated. On both sides of the divide, the cost of conflict drains resources, choked growth, and casts a long shadow over what could be a prosperous future for all involved. The assertion remains compelling: The economic burden of the Israeli-Palestinian conflict is a hidden casualty, its toll measured not in the currency of the realm, but in the lost potential of two peoples bound by history, yet divided by a ledger of unending expenses.

Infrastructure Damage

Amidst the lingering smoke and the echoes of conflict, the landscape tells its own story of sorrow the battered bridges, the ruptured roads, the shattered schools and hospitals. Once the backbone of societies, infrastructure in both Israeli and Palestinian territories has become another casualty, a silent witness to the ravages of war.

In the twilight of a ceasefire or the calm before another storm, the question looms: How profound is the impact of such destruction on the day-to-day life and future prospects of the afflicted populations? It's a question that leads us down a path of cold statistics and grim forecasts, but also of resilience and the human spirit's relentless pursuit of rebuilding and renewal.

The primary issue is sharp and omnipresent. Critical infrastructure in conflict zones power plants, water treatment facilities, and transportation systems face systematic destruction. These are not merely physical assets; they are the lifeblood of society, enabling trade, education, healthcare, and communication. When a single bridge is destroyed, it's not just a crossing that's lost, but a link in the supply chain, a route to school for children, a path to market for farmers. Multiply that by hundreds, and the scale of the challenge emerges from the rubble.

The potential consequences of inaction are severe and far-reaching. Without swift and strategic intervention, the economic aftermath can stretch far beyond the immediate recovery period. A crippled infrastructure leads to a crippled economy. Businesses cannot operate without reliable power and logistics. Hospitals struggle to provide care without clean water or access to medical supplies. Education stagnates when children cannot reach their classrooms or when those classrooms lie in ruins.

The solution to such a complex problem must be multifaceted, drawing upon international expertise, local knowledge, and a commitment to peace and stability. Investment in infrastructure must be prioritized, not just to rebuild what was lost, but to create a more resilient system that can withstand future conflicts. This strategy involves not only repair and reconstruction but also innovation and improvement.

To implement this solution, a multi-tiered action plan is necessary. Initially, quick-impact projects that restore basic services must take precedence. These serve as a foundation for more extensive, long-term development projects. International aid, private investment, and public funding must converge, guided by a clear vision and managed by a coalition of local authorities, NGOs, and international bodies dedicated to transparent and effective execution.

Evidence of this approach's efficacy can be found by looking at post-conflict success stories. In Rwanda, post-genocide infrastructure development has been a cornerstone of the nation's remarkable economic recovery. Investments in road networks and information technology have turned a nation once synonymous with tragedy into one of Africa's fastest-growing economies.

On the other hand, one must consider alternative solutions, such as decentralized systems. Instead of relying on large-scale power plants or water treatment facilities, smaller, community-managed services could provide a more immediate and sustainable form of resilience. Such systems could prove less vulnerable to targeted attacks, offering a continuous, though limited, provision of essential services during times of conflict.

Imagine a future where solar-powered streetlights brighten safe passages at night, where modular bridges are rapidly deployed to reconnect divided communities, and where mobile clinics cross-repair roads to bring healing to those in need. It's not a mere daydream, but a blueprint for a better tomorrow one that begins with the acknowledgment of today's challenges and the courage to address them head-on.

How will we navigate the road from devastation to revitalization? It begins with the will to see beyond the debris, to envision a society where the infrastructure serves not as a target, but as a testament to ingenuity and hope. It's the will to ask ourselves, not just what we can rebuild, but how we can build back better.

The story of war is etched in the ruins, but the narrative of peace and prosperity is yet to be written on the foundations of a renewed infrastructure. As the sun sets on a landscape scarred by conflict, it also rises on a horizon brimming with the promise of reconstruction and recovery. It's a story that continues with every cleared roadway, every restored power line, and every school that opens its doors once again.

The road ahead is difficult, but not impassable. With concerted effort and strategic planning, the long-term economic consequences of infrastructure damage can be mitigated. The resilience of the human spirit, coupled with innovative solutions and international cooperation, can transform the scars of war into symbols of strength. It is a path that must be taken for the sake of those who have suffered, for the economies that have faltered, and for the peace that still awaits on the distant horizon.

Trade and Blockades

In a world where economies are intricately linked, the imposition of trade restrictions and blockades can have far-reaching effects, extending well beyond the immediate conflict zones. The Palestinian territories, subjected to such measures, offer a poignant case study in the struggle to maintain economic viability amidst political turmoil.

The sun casts long shadows over the port of Gaza, where once bustling docks now stand eerily silent, the result of a blockade that has choked the flow of goods and the pulse of commerce. This economic strangulation has not only impoverished the local population but has also reverberated through the regional economy, affecting Israeli businesses and international trade relations.

The main players in this scenario are the Palestinian entrepreneurs and Israeli authorities, each maneuvering within a complex political and economic landscape. For Palestinians, the challenge is to sustain livelihoods against a backdrop of restrictions; for Israelis, it is to balance security concerns with the economic needs of their neighbors.

At the heart of this case study is the crippling challenge faced by the Palestinian territories: the blockade. Implemented as a security measure, it has had the dual effect of preventing alleged threats and, simultaneously, choking off essential trade. The blockade restricts the movement of people, goods, and services, leading to shortages of basic necessities, sky-high unemployment, and a plummeting GDP.

The approach to navigating these treacherous economic waters has been multifaceted. Palestinians have turned to tunneling, a dangerous but often the only available method to smuggle essential goods. Others have embraced technology, using the internet to sell products and services remotely. Meanwhile, international NGOs have worked to negotiate the entry of humanitarian aid and to develop local industries that can operate within the constraints imposed.

The results of these strategies are modest successes

against a backdrop of ongoing adversity. While the tunnels have brought in much-needed supplies, they are precarious and often targeted. The digital economy offers a glimmer of hope, with tech-savvy entrepreneurs finding ways to connect with markets beyond their borders. Humanitarian aid provides relief, but it is not a sustainable solution for economic development.

Reflecting on these efforts brings forth a mix of admiration for the resilience displayed and frustration at the systemic barriers that suffocate growth. The blockade has been criticized internationally for its humanitarian impact, yet it persists, a testament to the prolonged nature of the Israeli-Palestinian conflict.

This example of economic conflict connects to the larger narrative of the Israeli-Palestinian war, illustrating how trade policies and restrictions can serve as weapons as potent as artillery. They not only shape the battlefield but also the prospects for peace, as economic despair can fuel further unrest. One cannot help but ponder, what might the future hold if these economic shackles were loosened. Would a flourishing Palestinian economy lead to a more stable region, or would it introduce new challenges?

Through this analysis, it is my hope to foster a deeper understanding of the Israeli-Palestinian conflict's economic dimension and to encourage readers to contemplate the potential for trade as a pathway to peace. Could economic empowerment become the cornerstone upon which a lasting resolution is built? This question lingers, inviting us to envision a reality where trade and cooperation replace blockades and isolation a vision that requires not only policy change but also a shift in hearts and minds.

The story of the Israeli-Palestinian conflict is far from over, and its economic chapters are still being written. As we turn the page, it is incumbent upon us to recognize that beyond the statistics are people whose lives and dreams are inextricably tied to the free movement of goods and ideas.

Foreign Investment and Aid

In the Middle East, where historical grievances intertwine with contemporary politics, the role of foreign investment and aid has become a central thread in the economic fabric of both Israel and Palestine. Nestled within the aborigine cradle, Israel's economy boasts a robust technological sector, attracting considerable foreign direct investment (FDI). On the other side of the wall, the Palestinian territories rely heavily on foreign aid to survive amidst restricted economic opportunities. Here lies our central claim: While foreign investment and aid are crucial to both economies, they come with significant strings attached that shape and, at times, skew the regional economic landscape and political realities.

The primary evidence supporting this assertion begins with Israel's high-tech industry. In 2020 alone, Israel attracted around $21.7 billion in FDI, a substantial portion of which flowed into technological innovation. This infusion of capital has not only spurred growth but also positioned Israel as a global leader in sectors such as cybersecurity, pharmaceuticals, and clean technology. The tangible effects are seen in the bustling streets of Tel Aviv, where startups bloom like desert flowers after a rare rain.

The booming economy, partially fuelled by FDI, not

only creates jobs and prosperity but also leads to partnerships entangled with geopolitical interests. For instance, investments from the United States often come with expectations of policy alignment or military cooperation, which can limit Israel's economic and political autonomy.

Turning our gaze to the Palestinian economy, we encounter a different scenario. Here, foreign aid is the lifeline. According to the World Bank, in 2018, Palestine received approximately $1 billion in aid, equivalent to about 7% of its GDP. This aid is vital for basic services, infrastructure, and humanitarian needs, especially in the Gaza Strip, where the blockade has crippled the economy.

However, when we inspect this lifeline, we find it frayed with conditions. Aid donations from European countries and organizations, for example, often come with stipulations regarding governance reforms and anti-corruption measures. While these conditions are intended to foster transparency and efficiency, they can also interfere with Palestinian sovereignty and the priorities of its people.

The counter-evidence to our proposition might suggest that foreign investment and aid are neutral economic tools that do not inherently carry political implications. Critics could argue that these funds simply provide the means for economic development and that any attached conditions are standard practice in international finance.

A rebuttal to this perspective must acknowledge that while some conditions may be routine, in the case of Israel and Palestine, they are often deeply interwoven with political objectives. For instance, U.S. aid to Israel includes military assistance, which is contingent upon purchasing American defense equipment a stipulation that strength of the U.S. defense industry while reinforcing Israel's military capabilities.

Additional supporting evidence is found in the Palestinian Authority's reliance on aid for budgetary support. This dependence gives donors considerable leverage over Palestinian policies, which can lead to a subtle form of economic coercion. When aid is withheld, as has happened during political standoffs, the resulting financial crises can destabilize the already fragile Palestinian governance structures.

In conclusion, the assertion that foreign investment and aid are critical yet come with strings attached is reinforced by the evidence. For Israel, the influx of FDI has catalyzed an economic miracle, transforming the nation into a high-tech powerhouse. For Palestine, foreign aid remains a crucial support mechanism, yet it also subjects the economy to the whims of international politics. Both scenarios underscore the undeniable truth that such financial support is not just an economic transaction but also a tool of influence that can shape the destinies of nations.

Unemployment and Poverty

Amidst the lingering smoke of conflict and the echoes of diplomatic rhetoric, the stark reality of daily life within the Palestinian territories reveals a grim portrait of unemployment and poverty. The landscape, marred by barriers both physical and bureaucratic, has given rise to an economic quagmire, where opportunities are as scarce as water in the desert.

The Palestinian territories, particularly the Gaza Strip and parts of the West Bank, are riddled with unemployment rates that soar high above global averages. According to the Palestinian Central Bureau of Statistics, the unemployment rate in Gaza reached an alarming 45% in recent years, while the West Bank faced a slightly lower, yet still troubling figure. This issue is not merely a statistic; it is a daily struggle for thousands who find themselves trapped in a cycle of hardship and despair.

The impact of such widespread unemployment extends beyond the empty pockets and growling stomachs of those directly affected. It seeps into the very fabric of society, eroding the sense of community and fostering an environment where hope is a rare commodity. The streets, once bustling with the promise of commerce and lively trade, now whisper tales of what could have been, had peace and prosperity taken root instead of conflict and neglect.

The stakes of this crisis cannot be overstated. Each day without resolution is another step towards a lost generation, one where the potential of youth is squandered, and the health and well-being of entire communities are compromised. The long-term consequences of such widespread unemployment and poverty are profound, threatening to undermine any future peace process and stability in the region.

In a land where peace seems to be as elusive as a mirage, the fight against unemployment and poverty is one that must be waged with unwavering determination. It is a battle that goes hand in hand with the quest for dignity and self-determination. Let us not forget that behind every statistic, lies a human story, a story that deserves to be heard, and a struggle that demands to be addressed.

The Black Market

Nestled within the complex alleys of Gaza, a dimly lit warehouse throbs with clandestine activity. Here, the air is thick with the tension of illicit commerce, the kind that flourishes in the interstices of a society cleaved by conflict. This is a corner of the underground economy, an uncertain world of smuggling and illegal trade that has taken root in the shadows of the Israeli-Palestinian War.

The main players in this covert realm are as diverse as the commodities they exchange. There's Naveed, a former construction worker turned smuggler, whose livelihood was upended by the blockade. Then there's Sana, a pharmacist, who, in the absence of legal avenues, has been compelled to procure medications through unofficial channels for her ailing community. These individuals are bound by a necessity to a network that operates beyond the reach of sanctioned markets.

The challenge they face is twofold: Acquiring essential goods that are scarce due to the blockade and economic sanctions and then distributing these goods to a populace mired in poverty and desperation. The blockade, intended to be a measure of control and security, has inadvertently given rise to a black market that thrives on the unmet needs of the people.

Naveed's approach to this challenge involves a network of tunnels, an underground lifeline that snakes beneath the border. These hidden passages are arteries for the flow of goods: from food to fuel, from medical supplies to electronics. The strategy is perilous and fraught with the risk of collapse or discovery, but for Naveed and his compatriots, it's a risk worth taking to ensure the survival of their community.

The results of these endeavors are palpable. Medications find their way to Sana's pharmacy, keeping preventable diseases at bay. Electrical components power up workshops, enabling craftsmen like Samir to continue their trade. Even children's toys, banned from formal entry, emerge from the tunnels, bringing a fleeting sense of normalcy to a war-torn childhood.

However, the analysis of this underground economy is not without criticism. The black market, while providing necessary goods, also fuels a cycle of dependency and illegality. It undermines the formal economy and can, at times, divert resources from the most vulnerable. The ethical implications of such a system are a subject of heated debate, both within the territories and in the international arena.

This black market is not an anomaly, but rather a symptom of the larger narrative of the Israeli-Palestinian conflict. It speaks to the human drive to survive and adapt, even under the most oppressive conditions. It is a testament to the resilience of people who, when faced with a wall, will dig a tunnel. One must ponder, what does this say about the nature of conflict and its unintended consequences? How do measures meant to impose order often lead to the sprouting of new, disorderly systems of survival?

My diverse experiences have taught me that adversity often breeds not just hardship, but also innovation. The black market of the Israeli-Palestinian conflict is a sad example of this. While it may be easy to condemn or dismiss these activities, we must also strive to understand the human stories that drive them. It is within these stories that we find not only the seeds of current strife but also the potential for future reconciliation.

The narrative of the black market, with its complex interplay of survival and legality, forces us to confront uncomfortable questions. It challenges us to re-evaluate the impact of our actions and policies, and to recognize the enduring spirit of people who seek normalcy in the most abnormal of circumstances. As we turn the page, let us reflect on the resilience of the human spirit and the lengths to which it will go to forge a semblance of life amidst the ruins of war.

Chapter 10

THE ROLE OF THE MEDIA-
FRAMING THE NARRATIVE

*I*n the complications of human conflict, few puzzles are as intricate and enduring as the Israeli-Palestinian war. At the heart of this complex dispute lies a battle for narratives, each side vying to etch their perspective into the global consciousness. Media outlets, wielding words as their weapons, play a critical role in shaping these narratives, often influencing public opinion with the subtlety of a master artist.

Why does it matter how a story is told, and who tells it? The power to influence perception and, by extension, international policy and action, rests heavily on the framing of events. Our journey into this analysis is not merely academic; it is a vital exploration of the invisible forces that shape our understanding of a conflict that has burned for generations.

The assertion at the center of our examination is that media outlets use deliberate framing techniques to influence public opinion on the Israeli-Palestinian conflict. These techniques are neither random nor benign; they are crafted to evoke specific emotions and align with particular political agendas.

Consider the introduction of terms such as 'occupied

territories' versus 'disputed territories.' The former evokes a sense of illegality and oppression, while the latter suggests a disagreement between two parties on equal footing. The choice of words is our first piece of evidence, revealing the subtle yet profound impact of linguistic framing.

Venturing further into this evidence, we scrutinize the images accompanying news stories. A photograph of a Palestinian child with tear-streaked cheeks, standing against the backdrop of a demolished home, tells a story of suffering and victimhood. Flip the channel, and you might see an Israeli family crouched in a bomb shelter, their fear palpable as sirens wail. Each image is carefully selected to elicit empathy for the subjects and, by extension, their cause.

Critics, however, offer counter-evidence. They argue that some media outlets strive for balance, presenting both narratives with impartiality. They point to joint interviews, and panels featuring voices from both sides and dissect the claims of each faction. This counter-argument suggests that while framing exists, it is not a universal or unilateral practice.

Moving beyond the initial evidence, we consider the historical context provided in reports. How far back do the outlets go to explain the roots of the conflict? Does the narrative begin with the establishment of the State of Israel in 1948, the Six-Day War in 1967, or much earlier historical claims? This choice shapes the viewer's understanding of who is the aggressor and who is defending their ancestral right.

The conclusion we are inevitably drawn to is that media framing is an omnipresent and potent element in the dissemination of information about the Israeli-Palestinian conflict. The techniques employed are multifaceted and deeply embedded in the very fabric of reporting. The objective is not only to report events but also to guide the audience toward a particular interpretation of those events.

In the final analysis, the assertion that media outlets frame the Israeli-Palestinian conflict to shape public opinion stands firmly. It is a testament to the power of language and image, the authority of those who control information, and the responsibility that comes with such control. It is a reminder that in wars of ideology, the battleground extends far beyond the physical; it encompasses minds and hearts across the globe.

Framing the narrative is not just a chapter title; it is a reality that dictates how millions perceive a land steeped in ancient tales and modern bloodshed. As readers, we must ask ourselves: Through what lens are we viewing this conflict, and how has that view been shaped by the hands of unseen narrators?

Social Media Warfare

In the ever-evolving theatre of the Israeli-Palestinian conflict, a new front has emerged, one where bytes and hashtags carry as much weight as bullets and diplomacy. As the digital age matures, the role of social media in this enduring conflict has crystallized, revealing itself as a potent tool in the hands of those seeking to influence public opinion, mobilize support, and document abuses. This 'Social Media Warfare,' seeks to unpack the complexities of this modern battleground.

The sun had barely risen above the horizon when the first

tweet of the day was fired off. It was a simple message, but within minutes, it had been retweeted thousands of times. This tweet was the digital echo of a conflict that has spanned decades, and it marked the beginning of a day where the war would be fought not only on the ground but also in the virtual realm of social media.

The main players in this digital drama are as diverse as the social platforms they inhabit. On one side, activist groups and individuals use social media to shine a light on what they label as injustices and to rally global support. On the opposite end, official state actors employ social media for public diplomacy, seeking to sway international opinion by presenting their perspective on the conflict.

The challenge is clear: In an age where information can spread globally in seconds, both sides struggle to control the narrative, to ensure their version of events takes precedence. This is a war of perception as much as it is a war of territory and sovereignty.

To meet this challenge, each side has developed intricate strategies. Activists and grassroots organizations often employ real-time documentation of events on the ground, using smartphones to capture images and videos of protests, clashes, and the daily struggles of life under conflict. These are immediately uploaded to platforms like Twitter, Facebook, and Instagram, accompanied by hashtags designed to trend and garner international attention.

In contrast, state actors have created sophisticated social media units within their governmental structures. These entities craft campaigns that include everything, from infographics to character-driven narratives, aiming to humanize their soldiers and citizens while vilifying their adversaries. They leverage analytics to target specific demographics and tailor content to resonate with diverse international communities.

The results of these social media skirmishes are mixed. On one hand, there are undeniable successes: mobilization of protests, shifts in public opinion, and even policy changes have all been attributed to social media campaigns. On the other, the noise of conflicting reports and propaganda can drown out objective truths, leading to confusion and misinformation.

Reflecting on these outcomes, it becomes evident that social media has not only changed the way wars are fought but also the way they are perceived. The immediate and visceral nature of the content shared can elicit strong emotional responses, but it can also lead to snap judgments without full context.

Journalists on the Ground

Dust and debris danced in the air as the echoes of distant explosions punctuated the tense silence. It was a narrow street in Gaza, its walls scarred with the stories of countless skirmishes. Amidst the chaos, a figure moved with purposeful strides, a camera slung over his shoulder, the lens a silent witness to the unfolding drama. That figure was Daniel, a seasoned journalist, who had made conflict zones his home away from home.

Daniel was no stranger to peril, having reported from the world's most volatile hotspots. His eyes, a piercing blue, had seen humanity at both its most heroic and its most heinous. They say the eyes are windows to the soul, and his were like clear panes, spotless by the smoke of bias or the fog of indifference. He was here to tell a story, the story of people caught in the crossfire of ideologies and artillery.

The day began like any other; a cup of strong coffee, a review of notes, and a mental bracing for the day ahead. As Daniel moved through the rubble-strewn streets, his fixer, Ahmed, a local with an encyclopedic knowledge of the back alleys and safe houses, guided him with a hand that had too often felt the sting of shrapnel.

Why, one might wonder, would someone willingly step into the heart of danger? Daniel often asked himself the same question. But the answer was always the same: to shine a light where darkness prevailed, to give voice to the voiceless, to bear witness. Today, he was determined to capture the human side of the conflict, the stories that statistics and strategic analyses failed to convey.

What is it like, you may ask, to live a day in the shoes of those who live with the specter of war? It is a question that haunted Daniel, and through his lens, he sought to provide a glimpse into that reality. A mother clutching her child, a tear rolling down her cheek, a wordless prayer on her lips. A young man, face set in grim determination, as he refines through the ruins for remains of his life before the conflict. These were the moments that Daniel captured, the fragments of life that persisted amid devastation.

But then, the unexpected struck. As Daniel focused his camera on a group of children playing amidst the ruins, a sudden blast rattled the street. Instability, the ever-present shadow of the region, had once again reared its head. As the dust settled, the piercing cry of a child sliced through the confusion. Daniel's heart raced, and his journalistic instincts were replaced by a more primal urge to help. He dropped the camera and rushed to the side of a young boy, blood seeping through his tattered shirt.

At that moment, the war was no longer an abstract concept chronicled in news reports; it was painfully, viscerally real. The boy's eyes locked with Daniel's, a silent plea for comfort, for salvation. Daniel, with the help of Ahmed, carried the child to the nearest makeshift clinic, a place all too familiar with such tragedies.

Later, as he reflected on the day's events, Daniel realized that his role as a journalist was not just to observe, but to engage with the reality of those he reported on. His anecdotes were not merely tales to be told, but lives with which he had intimately and irrevocably intertwined.

What lessons can we, as distant observers, learn from such stories? They remind us that in every conflict, humanity is the common denominator. They bring us face-to-face with the complexities of war, challenging us to look beyond the black-and-white narratives often presented to us.

Through the eyes of journalists like Daniel, we gain more than just accounts of events; we are offered a mirror to our collective soul.

Censorship and Control

In the shadow of conflict, where the cacophony of ideological clashes drowns out the whispers of everyday life, there exists a silent battle a war over words, images, and narratives. It is here, within the heart of the Israeli-Palestinian conflict, that we find another front line, one that is defined not by the physical demarcations of territory, but by the intangible borders of information and expression.

In a world where the pen is mightier than the sword, the forces that govern the flow of information wield substantial power. While the power of censorship is not unique to any one region, in the context of the Israeli-Palestinian conflict, it becomes a particularly potent weapon one that can shape perceptions, influence international opinion, and even alter the course of political events.

The crux of the issue lies in a simple yet profound question: What happens when the freedom to report, document, and express is shackled by the chains of censorship? The consequences are far-reaching and multifaceted, affecting not only the media landscape but also the very fabric of society.

Suppose the voices of journalists, bloggers, and citizens are systematically suffocated. In that case, we face a future where the narrative of the conflict is distorted, where misinformation can flourish unchecked, and where the stories of those most affected are lost to silence. Under such constraints, the truth becomes a casualty of war, its contours blurred by the biases and agendas of those in power.

Confronting this reality, we must consider the avenues available to us to preserve and protect the sanctity of information. The solution, it seems, lies in the fostering of a robust and resilient media ecosystem one that can withstand the pressures of censorship and provide a platform for diverse perspectives.

The implementation of this vision requires a multi-pronged approach. It calls for the establishment of independent media outlets, the support of international organizations dedicated to press freedom, and the empowerment of local journalists through training and resources. It also necessitates the protection of digital spaces, where the free exchange of ideas is often most vibrant and vulnerable.

To glimpse the efficacy of such solutions, one can look to instances where the resilience of the media has triumphed over attempts at control. Independent reporting has brought to light stories, that would otherwise remain in the shadows, and the courage of journalists has paved the way for a more informed and engaged public.

There remains the question of alternative solutions. What other paths might we walk to safeguard media freedom? Could the international community play a more influential role in advocating for press rights? Might technology offer new tools to circumvent censorship?

As we ponder these questions, let us not forget the weight of responsibility that rests on our shoulders. With each word read, each image shared, and each story told, we participate in the shaping of history. The landscape of censorship and control within the Israeli-Palestinian conflict is a testament to the enduring struggle for truth, a struggle that demands our attention, our actions, and our unwavering commitment.

So, dear reader, as you turn the pages of this book, ask yourself: How will you contribute to the narrative? Will you be a passive consumer of information, or will you seek out the untold stories, the voices that yearn to be heard? The choice is yours, and it is one that holds the power to change not just the way we view the conflict, but the very nature of the world we live in.

The Power of Imagery

As daylight breaks over the scarred landscape, the air trembles with the echoes of last night's turmoil. The sun, a silent witness, rises over a tableau of destruction a neighborhood now rubble and ash. In this moment of calm after the storm, a single image pierces the veil of statistics and reports, an image that will soon travel beyond these borders, across oceans, and into the hearts and minds of millions.

In the frame stands a child, no older than eight, clutching a tattered doll a stark contrast to the devastation that surrounds her. Her eyes, wide and unblinking, seem to capture the entirety of the conflict in one haunting gaze. This photograph, this frozen sliver of time, is about to become the epicenter of a global reaction, as it is shared and reshaped within the narrative of the Israeli-Palestinian War.

The main players in this unfolding drama are manifold. There is the photographer, a local journalist who has witnessed the cyclical violence that marks this land. There are international media outlets, ever-thirsty for compelling visuals to bolster their news cycles. And there are the activists, human rights advocates, and policymakers, each interpreting the image through their own lens of agendas and aspirations.

The challenge, as always, lies in discerning the truth amidst the fray. How can one image encapsulate the complex tapestry of historical grievances, political maneuvering, and human suffering that defines this war? The problem is multi-layered, as the photograph becomes a tool, a weapon, and a plea all at once.

The approach to understanding this image and, by extension, the role of imagery in the conflict requires a meticulous deconstruction of its elements. The photographer's intent, the context of the moment captured, and the subsequent path of dissemination, all these factors unite to inform the narrative that emerges. The image travels from the photographer's lens to the world stage, where it is interpreted and re-interpreted, each iteration compounding its emotional resonance.

The results are powerful and immediate. Public outcry swells, humanitarian aid is mobilized, and on the global political stage, leaders are pressed to respond. Data shows spikes in social media engagement, shifts in public opinion, and even policy changes all stemming from the dissemination of a single, compelling image.

Reflecting on this case, one cannot help but ponder the implications. What are the ethical considerations of using such images? Do they inspire empathy and action, or do they commodify suffering? It's a delicate balance between raising awareness and respecting the dignity of those caught in the conflict.

Visual aids, like the photograph itself, serve to bring these questions into sharper focus. They act as a bridge between abstract statistics and the visceral reality of those living in the war. Through them, we see not just the physical destruction, but also the resilience and humanity of those who endure.

This instance connects back to the larger narrative of the

Israeli-Palestinian conflict, a narrative where imagery is a permanent tool in shaping perceptions. The power of a single photograph or video clip can transcend borders, languages, and cultures, becoming a touchstone for solidarity or a beacon for action.

I am no stranger to the complexities of war and the impact of imagery. I've seen the power such images wield. But as we navigate the narratives, we must always strive to look beyond the frame, to the stories untold, and the voices unheard. Only then can we begin to grasp the full scope of the Israeli-Palestinian War and the images that define it.

International Media Bias

For decades, the world has witnessed the Israeli-Palestinian conflict unfold across the pages of newspapers and screens of televisions, with each side accusing the other of distortion and manipulation. Behind these claims lies a more pervasive and subtle influencer: international media bias. The very entities tasked with delivering news have often been accused of coloring the facts, shaping public perception, and altering the course of political discourse. This critical investigation peels back the layers of these accusations, examining the intricacies and implications of media bias in reporting on the Israeli-Palestinian conflict.

The central assertion here is that international media has, at times, exhibited bias in its coverage of the Israeli-Palestinian war, which has influenced public opinion and policy worldwide. To substantiate this claim, we must first consider the primary evidence: The patterns of coverage that suggest a tilt in perspective.

A study conducted by the Media Research Center analyzed hundreds of articles and broadcasts, revealing a tendency to frame Israeli military actions as aggressive and to describe Palestinian casualties in more personal terms. For example, descriptions of Israeli forces often included words like 'occupy' or 'invade,' while Palestinian groups were more frequently referred to as 'militants' or 'fighters,' rather than 'terrorists.'

The language used in media reports is not merely a choice of synonyms; it shapes the narrative and, by extension, the audience's understanding of the events. The use of emotionally charged words can elicit sympathy or condemnation, often blurring the lines between reporting and advocacy.

However, it would be intellectually dishonest not to acknowledge the counter-evidence. Proponents of the media's approach argue that the coverage is a reflection of the reality on the ground. They point to the asymmetry of power between the two sides and suggest that the media is merely highlighting the plight of the less powerful. Furthermore, they cite instances where Israeli narratives have been supported by major news outlets, especially when reporting on rocket attacks and terrorism concerns.

In response to these counter-arguments, one must consider the journalistic responsibility to provide context. While it's true that highlighting human suffering is crucial, so is presenting the complexity of the conflict, including the history, the politics, and the cycles of violence that perpetuate it. By failing to provide this balance, the media risks perpetuating a one-sided view.

Additional supporting evidence can be found in the disparity of airtime and column inches given to each side's grievances and narratives. A content analysis of network news over a six-month period showed a significant discrepancy in the coverage of Palestinian and Israeli-led violence. This inconsistency suggests an underlying bias that favors one narrative over the other.

As we draw conclusions, it's clear that while instances of bias in media reporting on the Israeli-Palestinian conflict exist, the issue is complex. The media's role in shaping public perception and policy cannot be understated. It holds the power to influence international relations, humanitarian aid, and the very fabric of societies.

In conclusion, the validity of the claim that international media bias colors the reporting on the Israeli-Palestinian war is reinforced through the examination of language use, context omission, and the quantity of coverage. The media, as the conveyor of information, has a profound duty to deliver unbiased news. Yet, as we've seen, this ideal is not always achieved.

In the end, the pursuit of objectivity in reporting on the Israeli-Palestinian conflict is as crucial as it is challenging. It demands of us a commitment to scrutinize every story, to question every headline, and to recognize that in the war of narratives, the pen can be as mighty as the sword.

Chapter 11

THE ROAD TO RECONCILIATION-LESSONS FROM PAST PEACE EFFORTS

*I*n the entanglement of conflicts that have marred human history, the Israeli-Palestinian dispute stands as one of the most enduring and complex. The path towards peace in this region has been fraught with setbacks and setbacks for victories, each attempt at resolution weaving its own intricate blend of hope and disillusionment. The pursuit of peace between Israelis and Palestinians is not just a political challenge; it is a chronicle of human endeavor, echoing the worry and aspirations of countless individuals caught in the storm.

At the heart of this saga are the earliest origins of conflicts, tracing back to the early 20th century. Zionism and Arab nationalism grew in parallel, yet on a collision course, as both aspired to lay claim to the same geographical fabric. The Balfour Declaration of 1917, promising a Jewish homeland in Palestine, in contrast to the rising tide of Arab self-determination, sowed the seeds of contention that would sprout into decades of discord.

A chronicle of milestones marks the fraught journey towards peace. The 1947 UN Partition Plan attempted to delineate a two-state solution, but the subsequent Arab-Israeli War of 1948 led to the establishment of Israel and the displacement of Palestinians, a tragedy they call the Nakba, or catastrophe. The Six-Day War of 1967 saw Israel's territorial expansion and the beginning of the occupation of Gaza and the West Bank, further complicating the geopolitical landscape.

Cultural and regional variations in the peace process are stark. The Oslo Accords of the 1990s, symbolized by the iconic handshake between Yitzhak Rabin and Yasser Arafat on the White House lawn, brought the promise of Palestinian self-governance, yet failed to address the core issues like Jerusalem and refugees. The Camp David Summit of 2000, and the consequent breakdown, underscored how differing narratives and unmet expectations can derail even the most concerted efforts.

The recent Abraham Accords, normalizing relations between Israel and several Arab states, suggest a shift in regional dynamics, but the Palestinian question remains unresolved. The journey is rife with challenges, controversies, and turning points. The unilateral disengagement from Gaza in 2005, the ongoing expansion of Israeli settlements, the intermittent wars in Gaza, and the cycles of violence and retaliation all these elements underscore the fragility of the status quo. How does one reconcile the legitimate aspirations of two peoples bound to the same land?

One might ask, have the lessons from past efforts been internalized? The importance of mutual recognition, the necessity of a viable economic framework for Palestine, the imperative of addressing security concerns, and, above all, the need for a political horizon that can inspire both sides to transcend decades of enmity.

In the search for peace, the adage 'those who cannot remember the past are condémned to repeat it' rings with a haunting resonance. Delving into details, one uncovers a litany of moments when decisions, both bold and misguided, shaped the contours of the present. The assassination of Rabin, the Second Intifada, and the blockade of Gaza each a chapter in the annals of a history that is as much about missed opportunities as it is about the relentless quest for a resolution.

In this moment of contemplation, we pause. We reflect on the gravity of the past, the complexity of the present, and the uncertainty of the future. The lessons from past peace efforts are like beacons in the seas of history, guiding us toward the elusive shores of reconciliation. And so, the search for peace continues, a journey wrought with challenges, but sustained by the unwavering hope that, one day, the bells of harmony will ring through the hills and valleys of Israel and Palestine.

The Two-State Solution Revisited

In the shadow of history's lingering gaze, the Israeli-Palestinian conflict persists, a complicated knot at the intersection of politics and human suffering. With each tentative step towards peace, the specter of failure looms large, a reminder of the delicate balance that must be struck to foster reconciliation. It is against this backdrop that we revisit the contentious yet pivotal concept of a two-state solution.

The current issue at hand is the deadlock in the peace process. Despite multiple efforts and international interventions, the quest for a lasting resolution between Israel and Palestinians remains elusive. The deadlock is not merely a political stalemate; it is a catalyst for continuing conflict that threatens regional stability and the lives of millions.

To lay bare the consequences of inaction is to acknowledge a future marred by violence, human rights abuses, and the erosion of hope for generations yet unborn. The region, already a tinderbox of tensions, could see an escalation into broader conflicts, drawing neighboring states into a vortex of instability. The humanitarian crisis in Gaza, the systemic vulnerabilities in the West Bank, and the palpable fear in Israeli communities adjacent to conflict zones are but harbingers of a grim tomorrow, should we fail to act.

The solution proposed herein is a re-invigorated push for a two-state reality, one where Israel and Palestine exist side by side, sovereign and secure. But how does one sculpt such an ideal into tangible policy? The answer lies in a multifaceted approach that addresses the core issues: borders, security, settlements, the status of Jerusalem, and the plight of Palestinian refugees. Implementing this solution begins with international diplomacy, leveraging the influence of global powers to bring both parties to the negotiation table. A cessation of settlement expansion, coupled with economic incentives for cooperation, could set the stage for renewed dialogue. Security assurances must be ironclad, satisfying Israel's need for safety and Palestine's desire for autonomy.

The efficacy of this approach is not without precedent. The peace treaties Israel has signed with Egypt and Jordan stand as testaments to the possibility of ending protracted conflicts. Moreover, the relative success of security cooperation between Israeli and Palestinian authorities offers a glimpse of what a future of coexistence might resemble. Are there alternative solutions? Certainly, one hears whispers of a single, bi-national state or even a confederation model. However, these ideas, while intriguing, raise profound questions about the feasibility of implementation and the preservation of national identities.

A river of ink has flowed in the analysis of this conflict, yet the solution has remained as elusive as a mirage in the desert sun. Can we dare to dream of a different future? One where the olive groves of the West Bank and the beaches of Tel Aviv echo with the laughter of children un-burdened by the legacy of conflict? Imagine, for a moment, an Israel confident in its security and a Palestine thriving in its sovereignty. Picture bustling markets, joint research ventures, shared water resources, and cultural exchanges that knit the fabric of peace tightly. This is not the stuff of fantasy; it is a potential reality grounded in mutual respect and the unwavering pursuit of peace.

The road ahead is fraught with challenges, each twist and turn demanding courage and conviction. As history has shown, the impossible can become possible when enduring the resolve of those who dare to envision a new dawn. As we contemplate this journey, do we not owe it to the generations that will inherit this land to forge a legacy defined not by conflict, but by coexistence? The bells of harmony may yet ring through the hills and valleys of Israel and Palestine, but only if we collectively muster the fortitude to revisit and indeed, to re-imagine the two-state solution in the mosaic of the modern Middle East.

Alternative Peace Proposals

In the quest for lasting peace between Israel and Palestinians, traditional diplomatic efforts and negotiations have often hit a dead-end, leading to a cycle of conflict and despair. Within this complex fabric of historical grievances and contemporary challenges, there lies the possibility of innovative approaches. These unconventional ideas and frameworks for resolving the conflict are not just academic musings; they represent potential pathways to peace that deserve exploration and consideration.

At the heart of these alternative proposals is the understanding that the conventional two-state solution, while noble in its pursuit, has not yet yielded the desired results. Therefore, a fresh perspective, that looks beyond the beaten path, is not just welcome, but necessary. The following proposals are daring, each with its unique potential to reshape the future of the region.

1. A confederation model

2. A bi-national state

3. Regional integration

4. Economic cooperation frameworks

5. Technological and environmental peacebuilding

A Confederation Model

The notion of a confederation involves a loose union where both Israelis and Palestinians retain their sovereignty while sharing certain governmental functions. This model suggests that both states could have their own governments and policies, yet cooperate on matters of mutual interest such as defense, foreign relations, and trade.

The concept is not entirely new; it dates back to the days when the European Coal and Steel Community laid the foundation for what is now the European Union a beacon of regional peace and cooperation. Could the war-torn lands of Israel and Palestine borrow from this blueprint to forge a new beginning?

Evidence of such a possibility can be found in the Federation of Saint Kitts and Nevis, where two islands operate as one country while maintaining considerable autonomy. Testimonials from the Swiss Confederation also offer insights into how diverse cultural groups can co-exist peacefully under a single national banner.

In practical applications, this might mean shared infrastructure projects, joint tourism initiatives, or even a common currency. This approach could diminish the 'us versus them' mentality, fostering a sense of shared destiny among Israelis and Palestinians.

A Bi-national State

A bi-national state would theoretically eliminate the division between Israel and Palestine altogether, creating a single nation, where citizens of both Jewish and Palestinian Arab descent could live side by side with equal rights and responsibilities. This idea challenges the very notion of separate states and proposes a radical rethinking of identity and nationhood.

Critics argue that such a framework could lead to the eradication of the Jewish character of Israel, while supporters suggest that it could be the ultimate expression of democracy in the region. Historically, there have been periods and places where Jews and Arabs lived together in relative harmony, offering a glimmer of what might be possible.

Evidence of successful bi-national or multi-ethnic states can be seen in countries like Belgium or Canada, although the complexities of the Israeli-Palestinian context are admittedly unique. Testimonials from individuals living in mixed cities within Israel could provide valuable insights into the challenges and opportunities of such cohabitation.

On a practical level, implementing a bi-national state would require profound constitutional changes, guarantees of minority rights, and perhaps a new flag and national anthem that represent the diversity of the single state.

Regional Integration

Looking beyond the immediate geography, regional integration suggests that peace might be achieved by integrating Israel and Palestine into a larger Middle Eastern framework. This could involve economic unions, defense pacts, and political agreements with neighboring Arab states.

Models of regional integration can be found in the successes of ASEAN in Southeast Asia and the aforementioned European Union. These alliances have not only fostered economic growth but have also significantly reduced the likelihood of conflict among member states.

The Abraham Accords have shown that there is a willingness among some Arab nations to engage with Israel, which could serve as a stepping stone toward broader regional cooperation. The practical applications of this could include collective security arrangements and regional infrastructure projects that benefit all parties.

Economic Cooperation Frameworks

Economic cooperation frameworks put forth the idea that peace can be built through shared prosperity. By creating joint economic zones, industrial parks, and collaborative business ventures, Israelis and Palestinians could become economically interdependent, which in turn could foster peaceful relations.

Evidence of such frameworks can be seen in the cross-border industrial zones between Turkey and Bulgaria, which have helped to stabilize a once-tense relationship. Testimonials from businesses operating in these zones often highlight the mutual benefits that come from economic collaboration.

Practical applications could include shared technology parks in fields like cyber security or water conservation, where Israelis and Palestinians are global leaders. Such cooperation could lead to job creation and economic growth, which might lay the groundwork for a sustainable peace.

Technological and Environmental Peacebuilding

Lastly, peace could be fostered through joint technological and environmental initiatives. The region faces significant environmental challenges, including water scarcity and desertification, which do not respect political borders. By working together on these issues, Israelis and Palestinians could build trust and cooperation.

There are many examples of environmental peacebuilding around the world, such as the transboundary conservation areas in Southern Africa, which have united former adversaries in the pursuit of ecological preservation. Testimonials from environmental NGOs in the Middle East highlight the potential for cooperation on issues like water management and renewable energy.

On a practical level, this could involve joint research and development projects, shared desalination plants, or cooperative efforts to develop the Dead Sea region in a sustainable manner.

As we navigate between these points of discussion, the questions arise: Can we dare to envision an Israeli and Palestinian society that thrives on the bedrock of unconventional but pragmatic solutions? Can the olive branch of innovation be robust enough to support the weight of decades of conflict? The path to peace is often winding and fraught with uncertainty, but the journey must continue with bold ideas that challenge the status quo. Each of these alternative proposals offers a vision of what might be a future where the cacophony of conflict gives way to a symphony of collaboration and coexistence.

The Role of Civil Society

In the entanglement of conflict that is the Israeli-Palestinian dispute, the need to understand the nuanced roles of various actors becomes paramount.

Among these, civil society emerges as a beacon of hope, a grassroots force that could pave the way toward reconciliation and understanding. This chapter delves into the transformative potential of civil society, exploring how individuals and organizations below the governmental level are engaging in the heavy task of healing and bridge-building.

Civil society is composed of large elements, each with its unique language and lexicon. To fully appreciate the narratives and actions that unfold within this sphere, one must become familiar with a set of key terms, each a thread in the larger peacebuilding efforts. At the forefront of this narrative are terms such as 'dialogue,' 'non-governmental organizations (NGOs),' 'people-to-people programs,' 'reconciliation,' and 'grassroots initiatives.' These concepts are not merely academic; they are alive and pulsating with potential within the contexts of Israel and Palestine.

Dialogue, in this setting, refers to open communication channels that allow for the exchange of views and experiences between conflicting parties. It is a foundational element of conflict resolution, predicated on the belief that mutual understanding is a precursor to peace.

Non-governmental organizations are independent entities that operate outside of governmental control, often aiming to address social issues and contribute to the public good. In the Israeli-Palestinian context, NGOs play a crucial role in initiating and facilitating dialogue and reconciliation efforts.

People-to-people programs are specific initiatives designed to bring together individuals from both sides of the conflict. These programs foster direct contact and aim to break down stereotypes and build empathy among participants.

Reconciliation is the process of restoring fractured relationships and finding a way to coexist peacefully. It involves acknowledging past wrongs, seeking forgiveness, and building trust—a delicate and profound journey for any society marred by conflict.

Grassroots initiatives are actions taken by ordinary citizens, often without formal leadership or organizational structure. These spontaneous movements can be powerful agents of change, driven by the authentic desires, and needs of the people they represent.

To grasp the essence of these terms, one must link them to familiar concepts. Dialogue can be thought of as the conversations that occur at family dinner tables, where different opinions are expressed and respected. NGOs might be likened to local community groups that work to improve neighborhood conditions. People-to-people programs resemble student exchange programs, fostering understanding through shared experiences. Reconciliation echoes the process of mending a strained friendship, requiring openness and commitment. Lastly, grassroots initiatives can be associated with the local campaigns or volunteer efforts that many participate in to effect change in their communities.

Civil society in Israel and Palestine is not a panacea; it is, however, a critical piece of the puzzle a realm where the intractable becomes negotiable, where animosity can give way to understanding, and where the echoes of war can gradually be silenced by the harmonious chords of cooperation and peace.

The Future of Jerusalem

In the heart of a region steeped in millennia of history, Jerusalem stands as a city etched in the consciousness of billions worldwide. This city of gold, alight with the faiths of the Abrahamic religions, is the pivot around which the Israeli-Palestinian peace process rotates. Jerusalem's destiny is not just a matter of political debate, but one that resonates with the spiritual and cultural identity of people.

To understand the gravity of this city's future, one must first grasp what it signifies. Jerusalem is not merely a geographical locus; it is a symbol of faith, an anchor of identities, and a cornerstone of historical narratives for both Israelis and Palestinians. Its significance is as multifaceted as the city's own complex topography, with each community laying claim to its ancient stones and sacred spaces.

At the crux of this intricate city's status is its role as a capital, a capital envisioned by both Israelis and Palestinians as the seat of their sovereignty. For Israel, Jerusalem is the 'eternal, undivided' capital, home to its parliament, the deficit, and the manifestation of Jewish continuity and resilience. For Palestinians, East Jerusalem, captured by Israel in the 1967 war, is the heart of their hoped-for state, the place where they seek to establish their own capital. This dual claim is a fundamental challenge to the peace process, making Jerusalem not just a city to be shared, but an idea that must be reconciled.

Historically, Jerusalem's significance can be traced back to the biblical era, its name resonating through the chapters of Jewish, Christian, and Islamic texts. Its foundations' roots lie in the ancient Semitic word 'Yeru,' meaning foundation, and 'Salem,' associated with peace ironically naming it the 'Foundation of Peace,' amidst centuries of strife.

When we contextualize Jerusalem within the broader framework of the Middle East peace process, it becomes apparent that the city is both a keystone and a stumbling block. Resolving its status is not only central to any peace agreement but also symbolic of the larger reconciliation efforts. The city's future is thus inextricably tied to the region's stability and the potential for enduring peace.

Real-world applications of Jerusalem's status are visible in daily life. The city's eastern part, predominantly Palestinian, contrasts with the western sections, primarily Jewish. Yet, there are enclaves where communities co-exist, albeit tense and often segregated. The management of holy sites, such as the Western Wall, the Church of the Holy Sepulchre, and the Al-Aqsa Mosque compound, illustrates the delicate balance of interests, and the need for shared governance solutions in the city.

It is a common misconception that one side's victory must come with the other's defeat regarding Jerusalem's future. The zero-sum game mentality has fuelled conflict for decades. However, in reality, the city's layered identity allows for the possibility of a shared capital a concept that has been proposed in various forms, including special international status or a divided capital model.

The question thus arises: Can the threads of commonality that run through Jerusalem's history be woven into a shared future governance? Will the leaders and citizens of both sides find it within themselves to look beyond the immediate horizon of entrenched positions to a new vista of mutual respect and coexistence?

Imagine a Jerusalem where children of all backgrounds play in its ancient alleyways, free from the shadows of conflict. Envision a city that embodies the potential for coexistence, where the mosaic of cultures and beliefs becomes its greatest strength rather than a source of division. This is the Jerusalem that could be a beacon of peace that shines forth from the heart of the Middle East, guiding the way for the rest of the region.

As the sun dips below the limestone walls, casting a golden hue over the city, one cannot help but ponder the profound significance of Jerusalem's future. It is a topic that demands the utmost care in deliberation, a subject that requires not just political acumen but also a deep understanding of the human spirit's yearnings. The future of Jerusalem is more than a political puzzle to be solved; it is a testament to humanity's quest for a world in which our shared heritage becomes the foundation for our collective future.

The question remains, whispered in the prayers of the faithful and debated in the halls of power: What will the future of Jerusalem be? Will it continue to be a city divided by walls and checkpoints, or will it transform into a bridge of hope that spans the divide? The answer lies within the hearts and the hands of those who dare to dream of peace, and of a city that, true to its name, becomes the foundation for lasting harmony.

A Vision for Coexistence

In the pages to follow, you will not simply read about peace as an abstract concept; rather, you will embark on an intellectual journey to uncover a pragmatic blueprint for harmony, a vision where Israelis and Palestinians not only co-exist but also thrive together. This is not a utopian fantasy, but a tangible reality within our grasp if we dare to reimagine our approach to the cultural, social, and political fabric of this storied land.

How can one propose harmony in a land where the drumbeats of war have drowned out the whispers of peace for generations? I acknowledge the weight of history and the depth of wounds that both communities have borne. My assurance to you is not born from naivety, but from a profound belief in humanity's capacity for transformation, underpinned by practical strategies that have seen the light of day in other corners of our world.

Close your eyes for a moment and picture the transformation. Imagine bustling markets in Jerusalem, where Hebrew and Arabic laughter intertwine. Visualize the classrooms in Haifa where children of all backgrounds learn not just the history that divides them but also the shared human values that unite them. Conjure the image of joint innovation hubs in Tel Aviv and Ramallah, where young entrepreneurs collaborate across cultural chasms to forge a prosperous future.

This book is a commitment, a pact between you, the reader, and myself. We are not bystanders in history; we are its sculptors. Through the journey of these pages, you will gain not just knowledge, but a call to action. The life-changing potential of what you are about to read is more than an opportunity; it is a responsibility we share to sow the seeds of a peace that will flourish for generations to come.

Consider the cultural exchanges that must occur for mutual respect to take root. The shared celebrations, the joint mourning, and the collective triumphs over adversity can serve as the bedrock for a new social fabric. We will explore how art, music, and literature have the power to heal and unite, to give voice to the shared human condition.

The social dimension is equally critical. How do we foster communities that are inclusive, that celebrate diversity, and that provide equitable opportunities for all? My experiences in education have shown me the transformative power of learning together. The strategies I propose will challenge the status quo and require courage from educators, parents, and, most importantly, the youth who will lead the charge toward change.

The path to peace is laden with the debris of past failures. But let me share with you stories of unlikely alliances, of enemies who became partners, and of initiatives that have quietly sown the seeds for a future of coexistence. These narratives are the beacons that guide our way- examples that show us what can be achieved with tenacity and vision. There will be moments of discomfort as we confront ingrained biases and dismantle the barriers of distrust. It is precisely in these moments that we find our resolve and measure our commitment to the cause of peace.

Chapter 12

ENVIRONMENTAL AND HEALTH CONSEQUENCES- WATER SCARCITY AND CONTAMINATION

*I*n the parched lands stretching across the Middle East, water scarcity claws at the survival of communities like a persistent drought. The Israeli-Palestinian context, fraught with conflict and political turmoil, worsens this scarcity into a crisis that threatens the very fabric of life. Every drop of water is a contested resource, a precious commodity that could mean the difference between sustenance and starvation, peace and conflict.

Dive into the heart of this challenge, and one finds that the problem runs deeper than wells and rivers can reach. It is not merely a shortage of water that plagues these lands but also the specter of contamination. The water that does is often poisoned by pollutants, tainted by sewage, or rendered unusable by salinity. The question looms like a gathering storm: What happens when the very source of life becomes a vector of death?

The consequences of inaction are dire. Diminishing water supplies could lead to crop failures, livestock deaths, and the collapse of entire ecosystems. The specter of waterborne diseases looms large over densely populated areas, with children and the elderly at particular risk. Social tensions could escalate as communities struggle for control over dwindling resources, potentially igniting conflicts that ripple far beyond their origins.

Amidst the barren area of challenges, there is a wellspring of hope. Solutions exist, practical and within reach, that could not only alleviate the crisis but also sow the seeds for long-term cooperation and peace. Imagine a future where modern desalination plants dot the coastline, turning the abundant seawater into a flow of life that reaches every home. Envision a network of wastewater treatment facilities that recapture and purify water, transforming waste into a resource.

Implementing such solutions requires a confluence of political will, technological innovation, and international support. It begins with the establishment of joint Israeli-Palestinian water committees, tasked with overseeing the equitable distribution of water resources. Partnerships with global experts in water technology could bring cutting-edge desalination and purification methods to the region. Funding from international bodies would be the catalyst, turning plans into pipelines and treatment plants.

Evidence of success can be found in similar arid regions of the world, where desalination has turned the tide on water scarcity. In places like Singapore and Australia, technological solutions have not only provided clean water but have also fostered a culture of conservation and sustainability. It is this blend of innovation and education that could chart a new course for the Israeli-Palestinian water crisis.

One cannot ignore the multitude of alternative solutions that beckon consideration. Rainwater harvesting, the revival of ancient aqueducts, and the use of drought-resistant crops offer options. Each comes with its own set of advantages and challenges, necessitating a nuanced approach to a complex issue. Will the leaders and people of this parched land rise to meet the challenge, harnessing the power of cooperation to quench their thirst for survival and peace? Only time will tell if water, the source of life, will be the current that carries them toward a future of harmony and prosperity.

Air Quality and Pollution

In the shadow of conflict, the air we breathe becomes a silent witness to the loud below. The Israeli-Palestinian War, a theatre of prolonged conflict, has not only scarred the land and its people but has also cast a pall over the very skies that blanket them. Amidst the clamor of battle and the cries for peace, the unseen assailant of pollution wages its own relentless campaign. This analysis seeks to capture the conflict's impact on air quality, to chart the unseen footprint of war.

The air in conflict zones is laden with a cocktail of dust, smoke, and chemical pollutants. It's a stealthy by-product of the warfare, that ravages not just the combatants but also the environment in which they fight. Our claim is this: The Israeli-Palestinian War has significantly degraded the region's air quality, with consequences that extend far beyond the immediate vicinity of the conflict.

Concrete evidence for this claim begins with the particulates that rise with the rubble of bombed buildings. The collapse of infrastructure leads to the release of dust and asbestos, fibers once safely ensconced in walls and ceilings, now airborne and perilous. The particles are fine, often microscopic, and when inhaled, they penetrate deep into the lungs, leading to chronic respiratory issues and diseases.

Delving deeper, the smoke from military operations and burning fields clouds the sky, a visual testament to the unseen damage being inflicted. These plumes carry with them not just carbon but also a suite of chemical compounds, some resultant from the combustion of modern weaponry and munitions. The smoke's reach is far, its lifespan long, and its effects on health profoundly negative, exacerbating asthma, and increasing the risk of cardiovascular events.

Critics might argue that the region's air pollution is not solely attributable to the conflict. They point to the pre-war industrial activities, the everyday traffic, and the natural desert dust that has historically contributed to the area's air quality issues. Indeed, these factors do play a role, but the war acts as a catalyst, magnifying the existing problems and introducing new pollutants at a rate that overwhelms the natural and societal mechanisms in place to cope with them.

In response, it's essential to clarify that while pre-existing pollution sources are indeed relevant, the war has introduced intense and acute sources of contamination. The burning of armament stockpiles, for example, releases heavy metals and other toxicants into the atmosphere, which can persist for years and accumulate in the food chain, leading to long-term health risks.

Further supporting evidence comes from satellite

imagery and ground-level monitoring stations, which show spikes in air pollution coinciding with periods of intense fighting. These data points illustrate a clear correlation between the war's major events and the deterioration of air quality.

As the pages of this analysis turn, the conclusion becomes as clear as the skies once were: The Israeli-Palestinian War has had a marked impact on air quality. The evidence is as tangible as the dust that settles on the streets after a building's fall, as powerful as the smoke that rises from a smoldering tank.

The conflict's legacy is written not only in the history books but also in the very air that the region's inhabitants breathe. It is a stark reminder that the price of war is paid not just in human lives but also in the health of our environment.

Our challenge now is to look skyward, to the winds that carry both the seeds of life and the ashes of destruction, and to ask ourselves, "How might we cleanse the breath of a land that has seen too much blood?" The answer lies not in the realm of rhetoric, but in the commitment to rebuild and to restore, to plant the seeds of peace not only in the soil, but in the very air we share. The path to healing is long and fraught with difficulty, but it is as vital as the air itself a resource we cannot afford to squander. Can we rise above the dust and smoke to reclaim the blue above? For the sake of all who call this land home, we must endeavor to do so.

Waste Management Crises

Amid the cacophony of conflict and the rallying cries for territorial claims, a silent crisis brews in the heartland of the Israeli-Palestinian War. It is a crisis of accumulation, of refuse and detritus, where the remnants of daily life intertwine with the debris of conflict, to form mountains of waste that bear witness to the human cost of prolonged dispute. We seeks to unravel the complexities of the waste management crises that are exacerbated by the unyielding conflict, casting a spotlight on the garbage accumulation and the dangerous dance with hazardous materials.

In areas ravaged by war, the infrastructure for waste management, once a mundane civic service, crumbles under the weight of destruction. Streets, once cleaned by the diligent hands of municipal workers, now lie choked with refuse, as the systems in place to whisk away the debris of human existence have fallen victim to the harsh realities of war. The trash piles up, a metaphor for the unresolved conflict, each layer a testament to the days, months, and years of impasse.

Imagine living alongside growing mounds of garbage, the stench a constant companion to your daily struggles. Consider the risks as children, in their innate curiosity, play beside heaps of waste that may conceal sharp objects, bio-hazards, or unexploded remains of war. This is the stark reality for many living within the conflict zones, where waste becomes not just an environmental concern, but a sad symbol of societal breakdown.

The consequences of mismanaged waste ripple outwards, affecting groundwater, soil fertility, and public health. The accumulation of waste is not merely an eyesore; it is a breeding ground for disease, a source of contamination, and a harbinger of long-term ecological damage. The urgency to address this issue is underscored by the ticking clock of environmental degradation, which, unlike the war, cannot be paused or negotiated with.

In examining the waste management crises of the Israeli-Palestinian conflict, we uncover a facet of war that often escapes the headlines, yet directly impacts the lives of millions. This book is a clarion call to those who view the conflict from far away and a guide for those within it, seeking a way out of the clutter of garbage that war has left in its wake.

The journey ahead is fraught with challenges, and the opportunities to innovate and to inspire a collective movement towards a cleaner, more sustainable future. Can we envision a post-conflict landscape where waste is no longer an emblem of discord, but a resource for reconstruction?

As we turn the page to the past and look toward a future where waste is managed with care and foresight, we must remember that the solutions we seek are not just for the land, but for its people. They are for children, for families yearning for normalcy, and for a region that has the potential to flourish once the burden of waste is lifted. With each chapter, we edge closer to understanding and, hopefully, to a resolution that can emerge from the rubble, a beacon of hope for those who have endured the wastefulness of war.

Medical Access and Shortages

In the shadow of a conflict that casts a long and harrowing pall over the land, there lies a silent struggle that often escapes the eyes of the world. Within the noisy borders of the Israeli-Palestinian War, a crisis of healthcare access and medical shortages unfolds, its tendrils reaching deep into the fabric of the affected societies.

As dawn breaks over a landscape marred by conflict, the harsh reality of this crisis becomes evident. Checkpoints, like arteries of control, snake across the terrain, regulating the flow of people and goods with an iron pulse. Here, at one such checkpoint, an ambulance waits, sirens muted, the tension palpable within its confines. Within, a team of medics hovers over a patient, their faces etched with the urgency of their mission.

The central figures in this daily drama are the healthcare providers and patients caught in the crosshairs of conflict. The medics, a blend of steely resolve and compassion, operate under conditions that would daunt the most seasoned of professionals. Their patients, civilians whose only crime is to fall sick in a time of war, embody the human cost of the conflict a cost measured in pain, delayed treatments, and lives precariously hanging in the balance.

The challenge, as stark and as unforgiving as the concrete barriers they face, is the access to timely medical care. Checkpoint delays are but the tip of the iceberg. Beneath the surface lies a complex web of shortages of medicines, of medical equipment, and of the very staff needed to wield them.

The approach to navigating this crisis is multifaceted, with strategies as varied as the people devising them. International NGOs, local health ministries, and a network of underground activists work in concert and sometimes in quiet opposition to the prevailing powers. They smuggle essential medicines in the dead of night, negotiate for checkpoint access, and set up makeshift clinics in the heart of conflict zones.

The results, while not always measurable in the metrics

of traditional victories, are written in the lives saved, in the pain alleviated, and in the hope kindled. Data, scarce and precious, tells a tale of small triumphs a child receiving asthma medication, a surgery completed under the flickering lights of a generator, a birth untainted by the sound of gunfire.

Reflection upon these efforts yields a complex mosaic of courage and desperation, of innovation born of necessity. Criticisms abound of aid funneled into the wrong hands, of temporary solutions to systemic problems but the prevailing sentiment is one of dogged perseverance.

This case study, an example of a larger narrative, speaks to the resilience of the human spirit in the face of adversity. It highlights the universal need for healthcare and the dire consequences when it becomes entangled in the barbed wire of conflict.

A single question lingers in the air, a thought to carry forward: What more can be done to ensure that the right to health is preserved, even in the darkest of times? As we consider this, let us not forget that behind every statistic, every policy debate, there are individuals with names, with families, with dreams momentarily deferred but never extinguished.

In the chapters that follow, we will explore further aspects of the Israeli-Palestinian War, each thread contributing to this enduring conflict. But for now, let us pause and consider the plight of those seeking healing amidst the ruins and the enduring lesson that in war, it is often the most basic of human needs that become the most profound of human rights.

Mental Health and Trauma

In the heart of a land etched with scars of a long-standing conflict, hidden battles rage within the minds of its inhabitants. The Israeli-Palestinian War, with its cacophony of violence and loss, has sown seeds of psychological unrest that have taken root in the deepest recesses of the human psyche. Here, amidst the rubble of shattered homes and the echoes of wailing sirens, lies a silent specter of trauma.

The sun rises, casting a golden hue over the fractured landscape, but for many, the darkness of the night lingers, carried within. It is in this setting that our narrative unfolds, in a world where the mind's battle for peace is as relentless as the war outside.

Our main players are not the politicians or soldiers, but the civilians, the children who have never known a day without fear, the mothers who carry the weight of lost sons and daughters, and the fathers who struggle to provide appearance amidst the chaos. Their adversary is an invisible one: The trauma that has nested within them, manifesting as nightmares, flashbacks, and a pervasive sense of dread.

The core challenge they face is Post-Traumatic Stress Disorder (PTSD), along with a spectrum of other mental health issues. The symptoms are not merely individual concerns; they ripple through communities, shaping interactions, fuelling cycles of violence, and eroding the fabric of society.

The approach to this cunning problem varies. Some find solace in the shared experience of support groups, where words give shape to the vague pain within. Others turn to professional help, though therapists are few and resources scarce. Then there are those who seek comfort in creative expression art and storytelling become both refuge and revelation.

The results of these endeavors are as varied as the individuals themselves. For some, healing begins with the simple act of naming the beast, of recognizing the trauma for what it is. For others, progress is measured in small victories a full night's sleep, a day without panic, a moment of joy amidst the sorrow.

We analyze and reflect upon these personal journeys not to offer a one-size-fits-all solution, but to understand the sheer breadth of the war's impact. It is not just land and lives that have been torn apart, but the very minds of those who live it every day. Criticisms of the available mental health support highlight the need for more resources, culturally sensitive practices, and a long-term commitment to collective healing.

This case study, while deeply rooted in the particularities of the Israeli-Palestinian context, connects to a larger narrative of conflict and human resilience. It illustrates a universal truth that the wounds of war are not only to the body but also to the spirit. As we turn the page, we are compelled to ask ourselves: How can we, as a global community, better support the invisible recovery of a war-torn population? What systems can we put in place to ensure that mental health is not an afterthought in the rebuilding of a nation? But for now, let us carry with us the understanding that in the aftermath of conflict, the mind too needs mending, and the healing of a nation begins with the healing of its people.

Agricultural Impacts

In the fertile crescent, where ancient civilizations once blossomed, the earth bears the scars of a modern struggle the Israeli-Palestinian War. This storied land, filled with olive groves and date palms, whispers tales of generations past, but now, the agrarian heartbeat of the region falters under the strain of conflict.

Lush green fields sliced open by barriers, orchards shadowed by military checkpoints, and farmers who awake not only to the crow of the rooster but also to the uncertainty of whether they can tend their land. The primary issue here is stark; The conflict has severely restricted land access, leading to crop destruction and a teetering balance of food security.

The consequences of inaction are dire. Imagine, if you will, a once bountiful harvest withering away, the price of produce soaring, and the specter of hunger haunting the most vulnerable. It is a potential reality where malnutrition casts a long shadow, and the very cultural identity connected to the land withers alongside the crops.

But despair is not the sole tenant of this land. There are seeds of hope and ideas that, when nurtured, could bear fruit. One such solution is the establishment of agricultural corridors secured and neutral zones that allow farmers to pass and tend to their crops regardless of their nationality or creed. Think of them as veins through which the lifeblood of the community, water, seeds, and sustenance can flow freely.

Putting this into action would require negotiation, international oversight, and a commitment to peace above victory. The steps are complex, yet conceivable: Delineate the corridors, ensure their neutrality through UN peacekeeping forces, and establish a local council of farmers to oversee operations a body that speaks in the language of olives and figs, not politics and power.

The evidence for the efficacy of such solutions is not just wishful thinking. Look to history, to other conflicts where similar measures have allowed for the bloom of peacetime economies amidst the ashes of war. Consider the demilitarized zone in Korea, where nature has flourished, or the cross-border trade initiatives in the Balkans after the Yugoslav wars.

Of course, there are alternative methods too, like the promotion of urban agriculture to reduce reliance on contested farmlands, or the implementation of advanced hydroponic systems that require less space and can be established away from conflict zones. Each has its merits.

However, one must not overlook the cultural significance of the land and traditional farming practices. Can technology and urban farming truly replace the ancestral connection to the earth? This is a question that echoes in the heart of every farmer gazing upon their untended fields.

The rhythm of this narrative of conflict, consequence, and cultivation is not one of despair, but of possibility. For amidst the churned soil and broken branches, there is resilience, a stubborn green shoot that refuses to yield to the encroaching concrete of conflict.

Let us then sow the seeds of peace and nurture them with wisdom and foresight. In the end, it is not just a matter of agriculture, but of the very sustenance of people's future. And perhaps, in time, the lands that have seen too much blood will once again brim with life, and the only shadows upon them will be those of clouds, ushering in the rain that promises a bountiful harvest.

Conservation Under Siege

Nestled within this ancient landscape, where human conflicts have etched deep wrinkles into both land and society, lies a different kind of battleground one that pits conservationists against the ravages of war. This is a tale of those who strive to protect the fragile threads of life that cling to existence amidst the noise of the Israeli-Palestinian War. It is a narrative not solely of struggle, but of the indomitable spirit of those who stand as guardians of the earth's most precious gifts.

In the quest to safeguard the region's environmental heritage, a dedicated cadre of individuals emerges, ranging from local activists to international experts. Among them, a figure of particular note is Dr. Yara Abadi, a Palestinian ecologist, whose life's work has been the study and conservation of the majestic Palestinian painted frog, a species teetering on the brink of extinction. Alongside her is Avi Cohen, an Israeli ornithologist, known for his work with migratory birds that know no borders or barriers.

The challenge these conservationists face is monumental: How to preserve biodiversity when every day is overshadowed by the threat of violence? The environment becomes an unseen casualty of war, a silent sufferer of the conflict that rages around it. Habitats are destroyed, populations of endangered species dwindle, and the very fabric of nature unravels subtly yet persistently.

Their approach is as multifaceted as the problem itself. Dr. Abadi, with her team, orchestrates covert night-time operations to relocate frogs from conflict zones to safer habitats. Cohen, on the other hand, employs cutting-edge technology to track migratory patterns, ensuring that conservation efforts are informed and precise, even in the chaos of war.

The results, though hard-won, speak volumes. Dr. Abadi's initiative has seen a small but significant increase in the painted frog's numbers, a whisper of hope in a sea of despair. Cohen's tracking data has led to the establishment of critical bird sanctuaries, safeguarded by a rare consensus among warring factions who recognize the universal importance of these winged travelers.

Some argue that the resources funneled into conservation could be better spent on humanitarian aid. Others question the feasibility of long-term environmental initiatives in such an unstable area. I ponder these points deeply, acknowledging their validity, yet still convinced of the imperative to act for the sake of our planet's future.

These efforts, though localized, echo a larger global narrative, one where the health of our environment is inextricably linked to the well-being of humanity. In the Israeli-Palestinian context, conservation becomes a form of resistance, a statement that life persists in the face of destruction and that diversity triumphs over divisiveness.

And so, we're left with a lingering question: How do we prioritize the needs of nature when human lives are caught in the crossfire? The answer may not be straightforward, but it demands our attention. Let us then continue to ask the difficult questions, seek the paths less traveled, and honor the resilience of both nature and the human spirit. In the end, it is not just the conservation of species and habitats that we strive for, but the conservation of hope itself.

"The fight for peace and the fight for the planet are, after all, two sides of the same coin."

Chapter 13

LOOKING FORWARD-
PROSPECTS FOR PEACE

*I*n the heart of the Middle East, a land rich with history and soaked in blood, the Israeli-Palestinian conflict seems an ever-present fixture, a tragedy repeating with each rising sun. Generations have grown under the shadow of walls and the rhetoric of leaders who promise victories that seem as distant as the ancient stars above Jerusalem's storied skyline. But beneath the surface of this out-of-control conflict lies the faint pulse of possibility a chance for peace that whispers through the clamor of war.

The core of this enduring struggle is a clash of narratives, a battle for land and identity, steeped in historical grievances and contemporary fears. At the heart of the matter lies a mutual recognition of sovereignty, security, and dignity, a triad elusive in its pursuit, yet indispensable for resolution. Without addressing these fundamental needs, the cycle of violence perpetuates, each skirmish sowing the seeds for the next.

Imagine, if unaddressed, the consequences that loom on the horizon. A future where children inherit the conflicts of their forefathers, where cities crumble under the weight of endless conflict, and where the international community becomes ever more entangled in a web of regional instability. The cost of continued confrontation is not merely measured in lives lost, but in generations denied the promise of peace.

Amid this bleak picture, there shines a sliver of hope: The pursuit of a two-state solution, a vision where Israel and Palestine coexist, side by side, in peace and mutual recognition. The path is fraught with obstacles, yet it is this very solution that offers a pragmatic method to disentangle the knot of discord.

Implementing such a vision demands a series of calculated, diplomatic maneuvers and confidence-building measures that foster trust and dismantle the infrastructure of animosity. It begins with dialogue, a re-opening of communication channels long-silenced by mistrust. Following dialogue, tangible steps must be taken: the cessation of settlement expansion, the recognition of legitimate Palestinian governance, and the assurance of Israel's right to exist free from existential threat.

The Oslo Accords of the 1990s serve as historical evidence that, despite setbacks, progress is within the realm of the possible. Those accords, imperfect as they were, demonstrated that leadership when coupled with courage and compromise, can pave the road to reconciliation. And while the peace they promised remains unfulfilled, the framework they provided a phased approach to autonomy and mutual recognition continues to offer a blueprint for peace.

Some advocate for a singular, bi-national state, a melting pot of cultures and creeds living under one flag. Others suggest a confederation, a loose union of two entities bound by shared interests yet retaining sovereign control.

While these proposals present intriguing possibilities, they fail to address the core issue of national identity that fuels the conflict. Without a nation to call their own, Palestinians may reject a solution that dilutes their aspirations; similarly, Israelis are unlikely to concede the Jewish character of their state.

What is the path forward? It lies in the hands of those brave enough to dream of a day when olive branches may yet bloom from the barrels of guns. It lies in the commitment to hard and honest negotiations, where both parties can articulate their dreams and fears. It lies in an international community willing to support, not replace, the efforts of those on the ground.

As the sun sets over the ancient olive groves, casting long shadows upon the land, one ponders the fate of this sacred, troubled place. Can the rhythm of peace ever replace the cadence of war? Perhaps it begins with a single step a step not into the unknown, but toward the all-too-familiar dream of peace. It begins with believing that, despite the scars of history, the future is not destined to mirror the past.

The road to peace is long and fraught with challenges, but it is a journey that must be undertaken. The alternative is a perpetuity of suffering, a legacy of conflict for countless generations to come. Peace is not merely a distant dream; it is an imperative, moral, and practical necessity for the prosperity and survival of both Israeli and Palestinian peoples. And so, we must venture forward with cautious optimism, guided by the lessons of history and the promise of a better tomorrow. The prospects for peace are there, waiting to be seized by the bold, the visionary, the peacemakers.

Youth and the Future

In the vibrant streets of Tel Aviv and the bustling markets of Ramallah, a new generation rises, one that has inherited a legacy of conflict yet dares to envision a horizon of harmony. These are the youth of Israel and Palestine, digital natives forging connections that transcend the physical barriers erected by their ancestors. Their stories, often untold, are the threads from which the future is woven.

The sun had barely risen when I met with a group of young activists from both sides of the divide. Their faces, alight with the fervor of youth, were etched with a resolve that discredited their years. We gathered in a cafe that had become a clandestine nexus for dialogue, a neutral ground where ideas could be exchanged freely, away from the noise of the world outside.

Among these catalysts of change was Aisha, an Israeli student of sociology, whose research focused on the impact of conflict on childhood development. Beside her sat Ahmed, a Palestinian software developer, who used technology to bridge the communication gap with his peers across the border. Their backgrounds were as diverse as their aspirations, yet they shared a common goal to break the cycle of hatred and fear.

The challenge before them was colossal. How do you foster understanding in an atmosphere thick with distrust? How do you heal wounds that have festered for generations? These questions hung in the air, as palpable as the aroma of strong coffee that filled the room.

Their approach was both novel and audacious. They

sought to leverage social media, a tool of their generation, to initiate grassroots campaigns, promoting empathy and collaboration. They orchestrated virtual meet-ups, shared stories of daily life, and showcased initiatives that benefited both communities. They believed that by humanizing the 'other,' they could chip away at the monolithic stereotypes that had fuelled friction for so long.

The results, while not immediately seismic, were nonetheless significant. They had successfully created digitally interconnected narratives, revealing the common humanity that often goes unnoticed. A video series featuring young Israelis and Palestinians engaging in joint projects garnered thousands of views and sparked conversations that rippled outwards, reaching those who had never before questioned the status quo.

As I analyzed their efforts, I could not help but reflect on the broader implications. The work of Aisha and Ahmed, and countless others like them, represented a beacon of hope in a landscape often shrouded in despair. Yet, there were criticisms to consider: How sustainable were these initiatives? Could virtual connections translate into tangible change in the real world? These were valid concerns that merited further contemplation. However, the true power of their work lay in the human connections forged, a result not easily quantifiable.

Their story was but one thread in the larger fabric of the Israeli-Palestinian narrative, a tale of two people bound by geography and history. It underscored the potential of youth to act as architects of peace, using the tools of their time to build bridges where walls once stood. If the seeds of peace are sown by the youth, nurtured by their innovation and courage, what might the harvest look like? Can we dare to hope that these digital olive branches will one day bear fruit in the form of lasting peace?

With each story shared and each dialogue opened, the youth of Israel and Palestine are sketching the contours of a future where the past is acknowledged, but not allowed to dictate destiny. In their hands lies not just the potential for a ceasefire of arms, but a ceasefire of the heart, where empathy reigns over enmity.

In the end, it is not merely the grand gestures of diplomats that will carve the path to peace, but the small, everyday acts of bravery and understanding. As the sun dips below the horizon, casting a golden glow over the land, one can't help but feel a glimmer of hope. For in the courage of the young, there lies the promise of a dawn not yet seen a dawn of peace, of possibility, and of a shared future.

Technology's Role in Peacebuilding

In the shadow of past endeavors and the lingering echoes of economic strategies, there whispers another potent force in the quest for peace between Israelis and Palestinians: technology. This dynamic and ever-evolving field stands not only as a bastion of innovation but also as a beacon of hope, casting light on the obscured path to reconciliation. In a world increasingly interconnected through the web of the digital age, technology offers a unique platform for dialogue, transparency, and understanding essential components in the intricate mosaic of peacebuilding.

At the heart of the Israeli-Palestinian conflict, lies a web of mistrust and miscommunication, a barrier as formidable as any wall or checkpoint. The problem, stark in its complexity, is the rift that divides the narratives and experiences of the two communities. If left unbridged, this division festers, giving rise to a cycle of hostility that threatens to unravel the fabric of any prospective peace.

Imagine the consequences if this problem remains unchecked. A generation growing up insulated from their neighbors, their perspectives unchallenged, their prejudices untested by the light of alternative views. The digital divide, mirroring the physical, could deepen the split, entrenching ideologies and leaving the seeds of discord to multiply in the shadows of ignorance.

But what if technology could serve as the architect of a new dialogue? An open forum where voices from both sides could emerge, unfiltered and genuine, to share stories, exchange ideas, and build empathy. This is the solution that beckons a digital bridge that spans physical divides.

To implement this vision, one must first consider the infrastructure required to support such connectivity. Investment in broadband internet across both Israeli and Palestinian territories would lay the groundwork, ensuring that access to digital conversation is not a privilege, but a right afforded to all. Beyond infrastructure, we need initiatives that encourage technological literacy and innovation, including joint educational programs and incubators that inspire collaboration among young entrepreneurs from both communities.

Could the outcomes of such endeavors be as promising as we dare to hope? Consider the example of Rawabi, the first planned Palestinian city in the West Bank, which boasts a state-of-the-art tech hub. Here, in this example of possibility, Palestinians have the opportunity to work in a sector that transcends borders, contributing not only to their economy but also fostering a sense of connection with the global community.

It would be careless not to acknowledge alternative approaches. Some argue for the power of low-tech solutions, such as grassroots community building and face-to-face interactions. Such methods have their place, grounding us in the physical world we share. But in an age where social media can ignite revolutions and smartphones can access the vast expanse of human knowledge, to ignore the potential of technology would be to turn our backs on a powerful ally.

Pause now, and envision a future where Israeli and Palestinian innovation thrives in a shared digital marketplace. Can you see it? The exchange of not just goods but ideas, the collaboration that sparks breakthroughs in medicine, energy, and beyond.

This is not a distant dream, but a tangible, achievable reality. Initiatives like MEET (Middle East Entrepreneurs of Tomorrow), which brings together young Israeli and Palestinian leaders through technology and entrepreneurship, are already sowing the seeds for this future. They foster an environment where the language of code creates common ground, and the pursuit of innovation supersedes divisive rhetoric.

As we journey through this last chapter of the book, let us not forget that technology is but a tool; its power lies in the hands of those who wield it. In the right hands, it can dismantle barriers and build bridges. It can amplify voices that yearn for peace and spotlight commonalities that overshadow differences.

In the final analysis, it is the human element that will determine the success of peacebuilding efforts. Technology, with all its potential, serves as an extension of our collective will. A will that must be steadfast in its pursuit of peace. It is up to Israelis and Palestinians alike to harness this tool, to write a narrative not of conflict, but of cooperation, not of division, but of unity.

International Solidarity Movements

In an age where the digital realm has become a battleground for narratives and ideologies, there exists another powerful, though often less visible, force shaping the course of the Israeli-Palestinian conflict: the vibrant blend of international solidarity movements. These movements, composed of individuals and organizations across the globe, are united by a common aspiration to foster peace and justice in a land marred by decades of strife. They serve as a testament to the indomitable human spirit that seeks to transcend borders and barriers in pursuit of a world where empathy and understanding reign over friction and division.

As we delve into the narrative of these movements, let us cast our gaze upon a sad instance that encapsulates their essence. The year was marked by a crescendo of tensions, and the eyes of the world were once again fixated on the perennial flashpoint of Jerusalem. Amidst this turmoil, a coalition of peace activists emerged, a conglomeration of diverse backgrounds, cultures, and creeds, all converging with a singular resolve: to advocate for an end to the violence and a pathway to reconciliation.

The central figures in this chapter on solidarity were as varied as they were dedicated. There were seasoned campaigners who had weathered the storms of activism for decades, standing shoulder to shoulder with youthful optimists whose zeal was matched only by their conviction. Among them were eminent scholars lending their intellectual prowess, alongside artists whose canvases and melodies painted a vision of peace. Each brought to the movement their unique perspectives, but they were all bound by the shared belief in the power of collective action to effect change.

The challenge they faced was as complex as the conflict itself: How could they amplify the voices of moderation and coexistence when the cacophony of confrontation seemed to drown out all else? How could they navigate the treacherous waters of geopolitics, where every action and statement was scrutinized and often misconstrued?

Their approach was multifaceted, as dynamic and adaptive as the landscape they sought to transform. They engaged in public demonstrations of solidarity, their placards and chants piercing the veil of apathy that often shrouds distant conflicts. They lobbied policymakers, articulating the moral and strategic imperatives of peace. They organized interfaith dialogues, where the commonalities of religion and the shared values of humanity were brought to the fore.

The results, though not always immediate or quantifiable, were nonetheless significant. There were instances where the pressure exerted by these movements swayed governments to reconsider their stances, leading to tangible policy shifts. There were moments when the stories and testimonials shared by the activists resonated with the public conscience, sparking a broader discourse on the necessity of peace.

Reflecting on this case study, we glean insights into the potency of international solidarity, as well as the limitations that accompany it. Criticisms abound, with Skeptics questioning the efficacy of external involvement in such a deeply entrenched conflict. One cannot dismiss the incremental progress achieved, nor the seeds of hope sown by these acts of solidarity.

Connecting back to the larger narrative of the Israeli-Palestinian conflict, one sees that the endeavors of international solidarity movements are not isolated phenomena. They are threads woven into the broader fabric of peacebuilding, contributing to the pressure and incentive necessary for political progress.

My experiences have shown me that change is born from the willingness to listen, the courage to speak out, and the wisdom to seek common ground.

A New Political Vision

Step into a new era of possibility where the age-old Israeli-Palestinian conflict finds not just a ceasefire, but a resolution rooted in mutual respect, understanding, and a shared desire for a stable future. This book is not just another scholarly dissection of a historical feud; it is a blueprint for a transformative political vision that will empower you, the reader, with insights and strategies to foster sustainable peace.

Drawing upon a diverse array of experiences, from the strategic precision of military operations to the collaborative innovation seen in the boardroom, and the nurturing of young minds in the classroom, I have distilled a unique approach to conflict resolution. The insights within these pages are born from the crucible of real-world challenges and triumphs, and they promise to unveil a pathway to peace that is as pragmatic as it is profound.

At this juncture, you might wonder, "How can one book propose to untangle such a complex and enduring conflict?" It is a fair question, and skepticism is a natural response to the promise of something that has eluded many for so long. It is precisely through confronting these doubts head-on that credible and innovative solutions surface. My background as a soldier, engineer, educationist, and social entrepreneur has equipped me with a multifaceted perspective, enabling me to approach the conflict with a comprehensive understanding of its multifarious dimensions.

Envision with me a political landscape where dialogue supersedes declaration, where shared values and goals pave the roads that crisscross borders, and where the children of both nations can dare to dream of a future unmarred by the sounds of sirens and sorrow. This is the transformative journey I invite you to embark upon. Through a series of meticulously crafted policies and programs, we can ignite a shift towards a cooperative paradigm that addresses the root causes of the conflict and paves the way for lasting peace and prosperity.

By committing to this reading, you are not just absorbing text; you are equipping yourself with the knowledge to be an agent of change. The ideas presented here have the potential to reshape not just political landscapes but also the very fabric of society. They are a testament to the belief that when hearts and minds are open to radical change, history can be redirected toward a narrative of unity and shared success.

I have witnessed the power of transformation across various fields. I stand with you today, offering not just words, but a call to action. The strategies outlined here are not mere theoretical constructs. They are actionable steps, tried and tested through the crucible of diverse human experiences. This book is not the end of a conversation, but the beginning of a new dialogue, one in which each voice can be heard and each heart can find solace in the promise of a better tomorrow.

Can we dare to imagine a world where the historical enmity between Israelis and Palestinians gives way to collaboration? Where the walls that divide are transformed into bridges that unite? Where the language of war is replaced with the discourse of peace? This vision, once perceived as a utopian dream, is within our grasp. And it starts with the understanding that the political shifts required for such a change are not just possible, they are necessary.

The journey toward this new political vision will require courage, dedication, and an unwavering commitment to the greater good. But the rewards of peace, stability, and a brighter future for generations to come are immeasurable. As you turn the pages of this book, let each chapter fortify your belief in the possibility of change and inspire you to be a part of the solution.

The Power of Forgiveness

In the intricacy of the human heart, where the shadows of old wounds and the echoes of past grievances reside, there lies a potent force, a salve for the deepest of scars, forgiveness. This concept, often whispered in the hushed tones of reverence or shouted from the mountaintops of spiritual epiphanies, wields the power to untangle the complex web of emotions that bind adversaries in a cycle of enmity and sorrow. The journey toward a peaceful future, especially in the context of the Israeli-Palestinian conflict, necessitates a profound comprehension of forgiveness, reconciliation, and the healing of past traumas.

Understanding these key concepts is akin to holding a compass in the disorienting expanse of human conflict. With clarity, one can navigate the noisy waters of pain and resentment, steering toward the shores of mutual understanding and lasting peace. The terms to be unboxed are not mere words, but beacons that guide the way; they are forgiveness, reconciliation, and healing.

Forgiveness is the deliberate act of releasing feelings of resentment or vengeance toward a person or group who has harmed you, regardless of whether they deserve your forgiveness. It does not mean forgetting or condoning the wrongdoing, but rather letting go of the grip that the hurt has on your heart. In the context of the Israeli-Palestinian narrative, forgiveness is the individual's choice to break free from the chains of anger and bitterness that have been forged through generations of suffering and loss.

Reconciliation takes forgiveness a step further. It is the process of restoring broken relationships and building trust between parties that have been at odds. Reconciliation involves acknowledgment of past harms, restitution where possible, and a commitment to move forward with a new understanding and respect for one another. For Israelis and Palestinians, reconciliation offers a blueprint for creating a shared future, one where cooperation replaces conflict, and where diversity is celebrated rather than feared.

Healing, the third of these pivotal concepts, is the gradual restoration of wholeness in the aftermath of trauma. It is the journey toward wellness that can occur on personal, communal, and national levels. Healing requires time, patience, and often, the support of others. For the war-wearied lands of Israel and Palestine, healing means addressing the deep-seated wounds inflicted by years of conflict, creating spaces for dialogue, and nurturing the growth of empathy and compassion.

Imagine, if you will, the power of forgiveness illustrated through the story of a Palestinian mother who, after losing a child in the conflict, chooses to forgive the soldiers involved. Her forgiveness does not erase the tragedy, but it transforms her grief into a force for peace, inspiring others to consider the path of non-retaliation.

Reconciliation is embodied in the efforts of joint Israeli-Palestinian initiatives, where individuals from both sides work together on projects that benefit both communities. These collaborations serve as living examples that former adversaries can cooperate and coexist.

Healing can be seen in the work of organizations that bring together young people from both nations to engage in dialogue and shared activities. Through these encounters, the next generation learns to view each other not as enemies, but as fellow human beings with shared hopes and dreams.

These complex words, when linked to such familiar concepts, bridge the gap between the abstract and the tangible. They offer a lens through which we can envision a reality that transcends the current discord.

Forgiveness, reconciliation, and healing are not merely

lofty ideals; they are the very foundation upon which a peaceful future can be built. They are the silent prayers of children who have not yet learned to hate, the solemn vows of leaders who dare to dream of a day without bloodshed, and the enduring spirit of a land that has seen too much sorrow.

Dwell on these ideas, let them seep into the soil of your consciousness, and there, let them take root. For in this fertile ground, the seeds of a better tomorrow are sown, watered by the tears of the past, and warmed by the light of hope. The journey ahead is fraught with challenges, but the compass of understanding these keywords will guide us through the storms and into the calm of a new dawn.

The power of forgiveness is not written as a conclusion to the story, but as an invitation to continue the narrative with a heart open to the possibilities that forgiveness, reconciliation, and healing can bring. These pages are not the final word, but rather a beginning, a first step on the path to peace that can be read by all who have the courage to forgive, the wisdom to reconcile, and the compassion to heal.

This is our time to rewrite history, to heal the wounds of the past, and to build a legacy of peace. Join me, as we lay the foundations for a new political vision, one where the Israeli-Palestinian war is consigned to history books, and the future is written in the ink of understanding, cooperation, and shared human dignity. Together, we can turn the promise of this book into a reality.

The chapters ahead are unwritten, the outcomes yet undefined. But with each keystroke, each shared post, and each collaborative project, we etch our intentions into the vast expanse of possibility. Let us write a story that future generations will read with pride a story where technology played a pivotal role in the crafting of lasting peace. For in this digital age, the power to change the narrative lies at our fingertips; it is ours to wield with wisdom, courage, and the unyielding hope that peace is within our reach.

ABOUT THE AUTHOR

DR. JOSEPH K THOMAS

Army Veteran | Social Entrepreneur | Educationist | Global Peace Ambassador | Philanthropist | Investor | Author

Dr. Joseph K Thomas has essayed many roles in his life - an Army veteran, a corporate leader, an educationist, and a social entrepreneur. He is a soldier by choice, an engineer by profession, an educationist by passion, and an author by accident. He is a man with a humble beginning, his journey from the war room to the board room and then to the classroom has been an illustrious one.

Dr. Joseph brings different experiences and expertise from multiple domains starting from the Military, multi-national companies, educational evangelism, and social entrepreneurship.

He is the recipient of numerous awards and commendations including 6 National Awards and 5 International Awards for his service and contribution to the field of Education and Philanthropy. He serves on multiple not-for-profit boards.

Dr. Joseph's first book, INDIA: THE NEXT SUPERPOWER, his second book, CONMAN - IN - CHIEF OF CAPITOL COUP, his third book, INDIA'S NEW NATIONAL EDUCATION POLICY - 2020, his fourth book, TALIBAN 2.0, and his fifth book, RUSSIA- UKRAINE WAR, are Amazon's #1 Best Selling Books.

ACKNOWLEDGMENTS

My love and gratitude to my wife, Helena, and son, Daniel, for their encouragement and support throughout this journey. My wife has been indispensable in the writing process. She not only read the drafts of my work in progress but also listened through endless iterations of my thinking, always offering honest feedback. She was joined in these efforts by my son, Daniel, allowing us to share numerous useful conversations at all stages of writing.

My parents, Mr. K V Thomas and Mrs. Mary, for their devotion to their seven children and constant demonstration of love, even in good times and bad times. My mom always reminded us that difficulties in life are not constant and we will have a better life in the future. Thank you for keeping me rooted and grounded even after tasting success.

There are far too many people to thank, so every person who has ever worked with me, attended my webinars, or events, contributed toward my work, or shared my message in any capacity, I am eternally grateful to you.

THANKS

Thank you for reading my book!

I really appreciate all of your feedback, and I love hearing what you have to say.

I need your input to make the next version of this book and my future books even better.

Please leave me a helpful review on Amazon letting me know what you thought of the book.

Thank you so much!

Dr. Joseph K Thomas

REFERENCES

» https://en.wikipedia.org/wiki/
Israeli%E2%80%93Palestinian_conflict

» https://www.financialexpress.com/world-news/israel-
palestine-conflict-an-unending-saga/2252350/

» https://www.britannica.com/event/Arab-Israeli-wars

» https://www.bbc.com/news/newsbeat-44124396

» https://www.reuters.com/world/middle-east/
whats-israel-palestinian-conflict-about-how-did-it-
start-2023-10-30/

» https://www.who.int/emergencies/situations/conflict-
in-Israel-and-oPt

» https://www.aljazeera.com/tag/israel-palestine-
conflict/

» https://www.un.org/unispal/history/

» https://edition.cnn.com/middleeast/live-news/israel-
hamas-war-gaza-news-04-02-24/index.html

» https://news.sky.com/story/israel-gaza-hamas-
latest-middle-east-iran-live-updates-sky-news-
blog-12978800

» https://apnews.com/hub/israel-hamas-war

» https://www.theguardian.com/world/israel-hamas-war

» https://afsc.org/news/5-things-you-need-know-about-whats-happening-israel-and-gaza

» https://www.nytimes.com/news-event/israel-hamas-gaza

» Photo Courtesy

» https://apnews.com/article/israel-palestinians-100-days-photo-gallery-b37dd435701fa583b8f857e024dc39a5

» https://www.aljazeera.com/gallery/2023/12/25/photos-israel-palestine-war

» https://www.aljazeera.com/gallery/2024/4/1/the-destruction-of-gazas-al-shifa-hospital

The Best Route Your Story Can Take.

IndiePress

To publish your own book, contact us.

We publish poetry collections, short story collections, novellas and novels.

contact@http://indiepress.in/

Instagram- indie_press

Milton Keynes UK
Ingram Content Group UK Ltd.
UKHW050734180724
445674UK00016B/637

9 789360 455125